THE HISTORY OF
MAIDENHEAD

THE HISTORY OF MAIDENHEAD

BOB CREW

breedon books
PUBLISHING

First published in Great Britain in 2007 by
The Breedon Books Publishing Company Limited
Breedon House, 3 The Parker Centre,
Derby, DE21 4SZ.

Dedication

To Lionel Conroy of Maidenhead,
Colonel John Liveing of Henley-on-Thames, and Russell and Ann Pendse
of Chalfont St Giles (Russell formerly of Reading) – all Thames Valley
people with a fine appreciation of Thames Valley towns.

A catalogue record for this book is available from the British Library.

ISBN 978-1-85983-562-3

Printed and bound by Cromwell, Trowbridge, Wiltshire.

Contents

Preface

This book is written in the belief that local history in Maidenhead and Berkshire – as in any other part of the country – can appeal to a wide variety of different minds for different reasons, and not just, as it traditionally does, to the narrow interests of local historians, antiquarians and archaeologists. On the contrary, local history should be able to appeal to all sectors of the general public, to school children and their history and geography teachers, to university graduates and their history lecturers, to local librarians and museum staff, to journalists, tourists and men and women in the local pub, in all sorts of ways and for different reasons – from laymen to specialists, and from children to parents and grandparents of both sexes and all ages.

In other words, local history is *everybody's* subject – a family affair – and not just the province of the aforementioned local historians, antiquarians and archaeologists.

This is my belief and it accounts for the generalised broad-brush approach that I have taken in the writing of this work, which provides a general introduction to the key developments in the history of Maidenhead in a quick-and-easy read for busy people, researched from a range of publications and sources listed in the bibliography at the back of this book.

I am writing this for the kind of people who are interested in an appreciation of local history, rather than a serious in-depth study that digs deeper and deeper into a narrow field in pursuit of minutia and un-worked sources of research – such as one might do for a PhD – and for this reason there are things left out or simply mentioned swiftly in passing in these pages as I stick to my objective and avoid over-specialisation like the plague. On the other hand, there are a lot of things that are included that I have noticed are not included in other books, and I have certainly not neglected any of the essentials of Maidenhead's local history, all of which are to be found here.

Aspects of the town's development that are not to be found in this history include, for example, the local community's ecclesiastical history, and the history of those families, businessmen and investors who have made

Maidenhead what it is today, all of whom are excluded, not because they are uninteresting, but because they are not of general, popular interest and so are better dealt with in separate specialist-interest books of their own. Most of all, this is a chatty book about key local developments, several of which connect with the outside world, nationally and internationally. This is a book that is peppered with a wide range of fascinating and entertaining stories for readers to dine out on and to think on, which is how it seems to me that most people like their history, local or otherwise.

Although I am not an academic historian, I have studied English Literature at the University of London and worked in jo⌐ ˜lism for most of my adult life, so I am able to bring a combination of h⌐. scholarship and investigative journalism to the subject of local history. I am also a Thames Valley man, having been born and bred in Reading, lived in Caversham Heights and also in Maidenhead once upon a time (in the Altwood Bailey), and I worked in Henley-on-Thames for the Henley Management College.

In other words, I am on home ground when writing about Thames Valley towns, villages and people.

A quick word about non-historians who write history. There's quite a lot of them around, from politicians and military men who have made history, to journalists who have reported it and very often written the first drafts of history, and to men of literature who have turned to writing about history instead of or in addition to literature and fiction, such as Lytton Strachey and Hillarie Belloc and J.B. Priestley previously, and the journalist and author A.N. Wilson currently. History, like politics, has been generally regarded as too important to leave it only to the historians or politicians.

Even academic historians stray into other people's territory, as we can see from the present-day historian Simon Schama crossing over into art history on television in the new millennium, even though he is not an art historian, and shedding new light on art history in consequence. Everybody, in fact, has been having a go at history, all covering the same or similar ground and absorbing the same facts, and all doing their best to write interestingly about it, interpret it and arrive at 'a point of view', to quote Lytton Strachey, to whom such a thing was very important indeed. For me, analysing and interpreting history is as important as having a point of view, although one does inevitably arrive at such a thing before one is through. But the important thing is to 'arrive' at a point of view through logical deduction and interpretation, and not to impose it on history even before you have begun to study, analyse and interpret it, selectively editing it in order to fit one's point of view!

The point of view that I have arrived at – the logical deduction for which is explained in the following pages – is that Maidenhead has a startling rather than a striking history (see Chapter 11), and that there are many connections between local and national/international history that have not previously been made by local historians when telling the history of Maidenhead. For this reason, I have made it my business to emphasise these connections because I believe that they are important for a clearer understanding of local history. They strike me as being important because they demonstrate the difference that local history makes to us all today in the new millennium, and not least to the people of Maidenhead. It is Maidenhead's hitherto neglected national and international connections – not widely or at all understood – that make its local history relevant today, for reasons that I have attempted to explain in the writing of this book. It seems to me that I am, for my sins, breaking new ground here, and it will be interesting to see how this is received at local level, not least in the schools where there are local history projects to be done, and maybe in the history departments of local and other universities that may care to consider these connections.

It is against this background that I have consciously set out to write this history of Maidenhead as if it were national and international history, because in some ways it most certainly is – as are the histories of so many small towns throughout the country, of course – and I have taken this view as a result of analysing and interpreting the key developments in question. This leads me to believe that the best way of writing local history is in a regional, national and international context, making sense of it from all those very different points of view, and offering national and international perspectives in addition to the local perspective.

In order to do this I have made connections that local historians do not usually make – either because they do not spot them or because they do not consider them to be part and parcel of local history – and these are connections between local and national developments that interconnect, in turn, with international developments, all made with the object of putting Maidenhead in its correct national and international context while providing readers with an extra dimension of understanding. This approach also provides an opportunity to learn the lessons of national and international history when readers discover their own local history.

Because the world has become a global village and England a multicultural society, it seems to me that any local history is best understood these days as a part of that village and that society, as an integral part of its national and international habitat (in addition to its very important local habitat, naturally) and with a new perspective to match. Hopefully this raises the discussion of local history to a higher and more inspirational level than before – I shall be interested to hear from readers who beg to differ – and it invites local historians and the townspeople of Maidenhead to see themselves in a new light, while at the same time being reminded of the old light that continues to glow from past times.

If local history is to come of age and be taken more seriously in the modern world, then local historians need to push at its conventional boundaries and cast it, as and when appropriate, in its proper national and international context. It seems to me that this is a much neglected area, because there really are many connections between national, international and local histories that are not being made.

In the interests of a good story I have also included what may or may not be apocryphal about Maidenhead in addition to the factual – taking care to distinguish between the two – because the apocryphal is as much a part of the community spirit of any local history as the factual, and it provides useful insights into what people were thinking and saying once upon a time and why. The relationship between fact and fancy is not to be ignored if this relationship is to be understood. There are, in fact, some very amusing apocryphal stories about Maidenhead; stories to dine out on! All good borderline history. Another relationship between fact and fancy that is not to be ignored is the one between art and local history, and the difference that is made by the former to the latter. This applies to the history of Maidenhead, as seen in chapter nine.

Finally the processes and materials of history – and the methods of research employed – are always an inescapable part of history itself, and I have come clean about this in these pages as I talk readers through these processes, materials and methods while also telling them the history of their town. How history is sourced and researched is a matter of importance to those who read it. It is the intriguing story of how the story is processed and put together! To include this in the telling of history can only add value.

Bob Crew
London
November 2006

CHAPTER ONE

A Wooden Bridge and an Elusive Maiden

The essential history of Maidenhead is a story of a 13th-century wooden bridge and an elusive maiden, without which there would have been no Maidenhead in Berkshire today, and no such name would have been given to the former hamlet that turned itself into a village that then proceeded to turn itself into a town, which grew up around this pioneering bridge.

It's as simple and magical (and as startling and enterprising) as that. But there is, of course, more to it than that.

Maidenhead may not have a great deal of history compared with bigger Berkshire towns such as Reading – where many more weighty things of historical significance have happened – which is presumably why the town has resisted having a museum of history to this day, but the history to which Maidenhead can lay claim is certainly startling, as we shall see from the following pages.

Towns and villages make history, either because of the actions of the people who were born and brought up in them, or because of the actions of outsiders who went there. Most of Maidenhead's history is due to the latter, although it is entirely due to the former that a small country town existed in the first place and so set the stage for the bigger things to be done, things from which history could be made in the fullness of time.

The town started off as an upstart community in the sleepy parishes of Bray and Cookham, and it was resented by both before breaking away from and outgrowing these places. The community was largely in Bray, which can lay claim to being the mother of Maidenhead in that sense, and it was a community that became a thriving little town in its own right that gave the phrase 'cock and bull story' to the world, as we shall see in this chapter. It was resented by Bray and Cookham because the parish churches of those boroughs did not want to lose parishioners, worshippers and business to a new community down the road, called Maidenhead – the place name of which has given rise to an eternal dispute about a mystery maiden and where she may have came from.

The *Oxford Names Companion* once reckoned that Maidenhead meant 'Landing Place of the Maidens' from Old English (1202), but this is very far from certain, as anyone who has taken the trouble to research this subject knows, and as we shall see in chapter five of this book. There are a goodly number of things that are far from certain when piecing together the incomplete jigsaw of any local history – and Maidenhead is no exception – and this is because records are either non-existent, incomplete or written in a way that does not quite add up. As J. Wesley Walker in his 1930s *A History of Maidenhead* has pointed out, there have been inaccuracies handed down from one generation to the next in the telling of the history of the town. He reminds us that there was a time when local people were taught that King Edward III – rather than Queen Elizabeth I – granted Maidenhead its first charter of incorporation (we shall come to this in chapter three – it was Queen Elizabeth I, not King Edward III), that Queen Margaret founded the Chapel of St Mary's and the Vicar of Hurley was paid extra for having to brave the dangers of Maidenhead Thicket, all of which were 'inaccuracies' that Wesley Walker claimed to have 'laid to rest' in his 1930s history.

It is not unusual for inaccuracies to creep into the recording and subsequent telling of local history, because items of evidence surface from time to time to contradict what seemed likely or was supposed before. The inaccuracies come with the territory and are the bane of a local historian's life.

Even so, one can usually be reasonably certain about enough things to get a useful picture together, and there are also such matters as logical probabilities and deductive logic that have a part to play, hence the use of such words as 'probable, presumably, reportedly, it would seem' etc, in the pages of those local history books that have got wise to the problem of uncertainty; it is in this spirit that a local historian makes his or her way.

There are many theories about what is the origin of, or what was meant by, the name Maidenhead, each and every one of which will be looked at before we are through, but when they have all been looked at we are still very far from clear where this place name came from and what it is supposed to mean, all of which lends to the mystery and charm of this ancient riverside town in the modern world.

For readers who are not familiar with the Thames Valley, where we find Maidenhead, a word about its scenic beauty. It really is one of the most beautiful spots in the country, stretching from London in the east to Oxford at the other end, beginning with Maidenhead, where Boulter's Lock is the traditional gateway to the Thames from here on, including the riverside towns and villages of Windsor, Eton, Bray, Cookham, Marlow, Henley-on-Thames, Sonning, Reading, Caversham, Pangbourne, Goring, Streatley, Wallingford and Oxford, to mention but a few. While Reading and Maidenhead are not as peaceful or as beautiful as they used to be – having had the spoiling finger of time and modernity upon them more than others – the remainder continue to sparkle like diamonds in a traditional necklace, and not least the more fashionable places such as the university city of Oxford, Sonning, Windsor, Eton, Henley-on-Thames, Marlow, Cookham and Bray. Thames Valley country is agricultural and farming country, with light industry and financial services elsewhere, especially in Reading and to a lesser extent in Maidenhead.

This is the landscape and surrounding countryside in which we find Maidenhead in the county of Royal Berkshire (where we also find such places at Royal Windsor and Royal Ascot).

Like so many other places, there are ghosts round every corner in Maidenhead, and with the exception of Maidenhead Thicket – with its notorious highwaymen and robbers – it would seem that they have been mostly good ghosts that have gone into the making of this town. Even the highwaymen may not have been all that bad because, as we know from so many history books, quite a number of English highwaymen are said to have apologised to the passengers they robbed in their horse-drawn coaches for the fact that their poverty had reduced them to such a crime. This is according to some passengers, both foreign and English, who have recorded these things in their diaries (but there is no record, alas, of the treatment of those other passengers who were not handled so well, who did not record such things in their diaries).

Maidenhead is said to have been the meeting place of King Charles I and his children before he was executed during England's Civil War between the Roundheads and Cavaliers, and the town also set the scene for an amusing and clever prank that was reportedly played on two members of the local clergy by King James I, who is supposed to have strolled into Maidenhead's Bear Inn back in the 16th century, following a hunting expedition, and asked if he could dine there, having got lost from his royal hunting party.

The Bear Inn in those days was situated at what has become 35 Maidenhead High Street in the 21st century, and it was an upmarket inn for the cavalry officer class (just as, in later years, the fashionable Skindle's Hotel in Maidenhead was popular with the officer class – particularly Guards Officers from nearby Windsor and down from London – in the 1950s and 60s). The vicar of Bray was rather full of himself because he was a man of considerable influence who expected to be treated as such, quite a local celebrity in fact (as a goodly number of ecclesiasticals were, throughout the land, once upon a time), so this was an inn with a good reputation that the King of England had happened upon.

Not recognising this huntsman as the king, in those far-off days before press photography and television, the innkeeper replied that the huntsman was not properly dressed and that there was no place at table, which had been taken by the Vicar of Bray and his curate. The huntsman replied that there was no reason why the innkeeper could not ask the vicar and his curate if they would care to invite a hungry gentleman to their table, who would be much obliged for a bite to eat, having been out hunting all day.

Being Christian gentlemen, the vicar and his curate did the Christian thing and tolerated the huntsman at their table, whose company they enjoyed throughout their meal, but when the time came to pay the bill and, to their astonishment, the huntsman let it be known that he had forgotten he had come out without any money, eyebrows were raised.

The huntsman was humbled, and he asked if these fine Christian gentlemen could kindly pay for his share of the meal and allow him to repay them in due course, but the vicar was not amused, as he glared daggers at the intruder, letting it be known that, in his opinion, there was no such thing as a free lunch and that he did not approve of freeloaders. So he said that he would not lend a single penny to pay for this impudent gate-crasher's meal.

But the kindly curate, on the other hand, took a more sympathetic and philosophical view and said that this sort of embarrassment could happen to anybody, and he would gladly pay for the huntsman's meal since he was obviously a fine English gentleman, who had been such charming and witty company (or words to that effect, I was not a fly on the wall).

The huntsman thanked the curate for being so gracious and considerate, and said that he would most certainly repay him with interest, whereupon there was a great blowing of horns in the courtyard outside the Bear Inn, heralding the arrival of the king's men who had come looking for him. When they entered the dining room and presented themselves, addressing the huntsman as 'your majesty', it of course dawned on the vicar of Bray that he had dropped an almighty clanger, and so, being the grovelling little vicar that he was, he immediately begged the forgiveness of King James I, and forgive him the king did, telling him not to worry, that he would not be locked up in the Tower of London or burnt at the stake in Windsor, and that he could keep his job as the Vicar of Bray.

But the king also added that the kindly curate would be promoted above the vicar into the Canonry of Windsor, for which, as it happened, there was a vacancy that might otherwise have gone to the vicar – had he not been such a mean-spirited and un-Christian skinflint.

This story – apocryphal or otherwise – is too good not to be included in any history of Maidenhead. The moral of the story alone is worthy of inclusion in any history, as is the entertainment value. This is a perfectly splendid, tongue-in-cheek story, so never mind the factual details!

It is a story that has been handed down from one history book to another – retold on this occasion in my own inimitable style – and we do know that King James I of England and VI of Scotland (son of Mary Queen of Scots) had a sense of humour. He is said to have quadrupled the income of William Shakespeare and his company when he came to power. He also introduced his own version of the bible, and he certainly hunted a lot in the neighbourhood of Maidenhead, giving oak trees from his royal estates for the upkeep and repair of Maidenhead's wooden bridge across the river. Whether he, the innkeeper or the curate invented or exaggerated this story, nobody knows. Whether it was made up because there were people who could not stand the Vicar of Bray, nobody knows, but it became a part of the folklore of Maidenhead and a hard story for the vicar to live down.

We are told in *The Hollow Crown* that King James I was 'very witty' and that he had 'as many witty jests as any man', so this clever prank sounds exactly the sort of thing that he might have got up to in Maidenhead's Bear Inn. We are also told that he kept a grave unsmiling face when teasing people and having them on, pretending to be serious when he was, in fact, being mischievous. Liberal-minded, crafty and cunning, we understand that he only 'appeared' to be religious and that he loved to party and have masques and formal balls at court, like Queen Elizabeth I before him. So the chances are that he would have enjoyed making fun of the priesthood when the occasion presented itself, as he seems to have done in the Bear Inn.

I don't know about you, but on balance I am inclined to believe this story out of Maidenhead about King James I and the Vicar of Bray, not that the vicar in this historical tale could have been the legendary Vicar of Bray, who was notorious during the time of King Henry VIII and Queen Elizabeth I and was well-known as a turncoat vicar. That one seems to have retired or died in 1565 or 1588, before James I came to power in 1603, and we are told that his name was Simon Symonds (although other sources give him the surname Aleyn), according to Wesley Walker in his *History of Maidenhead*, who also tells us that he was succeeded by Simon Dollin in 1565. The legendary vicar was celebrated as a truly vivacious and versatile vicar, who started life as a Papist, then became a Protestant, then a Papist again, having seen martyrs burn to death at Windsor for their religious belief and not fancying the same fate himself. Amusing ditties and ballads were written about the ease with which this man of God changed sides, but his reply was simply that he had always kept his principle – to live and die the Vicar of Bray, which he did: 'And this law that I'll maintain until my dying day, sir, that whatever king shall reign, I'll be the Vicar of Bray, sir.'

Because this vicar had captured the public's imagination far and wide –
and he was generally regarded as a bit of a joke because people just loved to
poke fun at him – it is entirely possible that his successor (about whom the
King James story was told at the Bear Inn in Maidenhead) became confused
with his notorious predecessor in the fullness of time when people told and
re-told this story. It is also entirely possible that a great many people liked
to make up stories about the legendary Vicar of Bray – as opposed to the
one in the King James story – even after he was dead! It's not as if they could
turn on their television screens or receive daily newspapers through their
letter boxes in order to know that he was dead, or even find out what he
looked like. In fact, Maidenhead did not get its own local newspaper until
1869. This was the *Maidenhead Advertiser*, ably assisted, before long, by a local
businessman called F.G. Baylis, who stepped in to make the paper the success
that it still is today. (Previously the town had been relying on the *Reading
Mercury*, *Windsor Express* and *South Bucks Free Press* for its local news.)

When we travel back in time, into centuries long gone, we find that the
air is thick with such stories and folklore, wherever we go, and not least in
Maidenhead where there are other stories yet.

Queen Elizabeth I – who granted Maidenhead the status of township
when she issued it a royal charter in 1582 – had, apparently, never been to
Maidenhead, but she had been to nearby Bisham Abbey, both as a child
under house arrest during the days of Queen 'Bloody' Mary – her Catholic
half-sister who kept her locked up at Bisham – and later on in her adult life,
when she returned to Bisham, a decade after she had granted her royal
charter to Maidenhead, as Queen of England. This was when she held court
at Bisham during the summer months of 1592. She not only conducted the
business of government from Bisham Abbey but held colourful parties and
masques there, while also discussing the subject of Sir Walter Raleigh having
made one of her chambermaids pregnant! She is supposed to have planted
a long-life mulberry tree in the grounds of the abbey for good luck. During
her recent Golden Jubilee Celebrations, Queen Elizabeth II paid a visit to
Bisham Abbey. One can imagine the impact on Maidenhead of the entire
royal court and government transferring itself from London to Bisham in
the 16th century.

In the 17th century, it was on 16 July 1647 that King Charles I, having lost the English Civil War against Oliver Cromwell and his roundheads – who was under house arrest at Caversham House near Reading – was taken to the Greyhound Inn in Maidenhead High Street for a rendezvous with his three young children (Elizabeth, James and Henry) before going on to London to be executed by beheading, two years later, on 30 January 1649, after he had been tried and found guilty of treason at Westminster Hall.

The civil war was the result of his adherence to the Divine Right of Kings – he levied taxes without the consent of his parliament, which he too often overruled and ignored, treating it with contempt and ruling without it for a couple of years – and also as a result of his favouring Catholicism over Protestantism (his parliament was protestant). When he attempted, unsuccessfully, to arrest five members of the House of Commons because his parliament demanded far-reaching reforms, this triggered a civil war, with Oliver Cromwell emerging with his roundhead army that took on Charles and his cavaliers.

When King Charles was brought to Maidenhead to meet his children, Oliver Cromwell reportedly watched them from an upstairs window. Oliver Cromwell was a Protestant soldier, statesmen (MP for Huntingdon), country gentleman and farmer, much in favour of religious toleration, allowing the Jews to return to England in 1656 after they had been kicked out previously, and he was not impressed by the Catholic intolerance of Protestants and others whenever a Catholic ruler was in power. He turned down parliament's offer of the English Crown in 1657, when he could have become King Oliver I, had he so wished, another emperor in the style of Napoleon Bonaparte. When the Scots invaded England – having done a deal with King Charles to restore the Catholic king to his throne – Cromwell had them in full flight and took 'thousands of prisoners', according to history professor John Adair, who tells us in the aforementioned book, *By the Sword Divided*, that King Charles represented the return of popery to England, which would have meant an end to Protestant and parliamentary liberties.

The National Westminster Bank stands in Maidenhead High Street today where the old Greyhound Inn stood back then, and there is a plaque on the wall recording this meeting between King Charles and his children.

Those were the days when it was forbidden to ride a horse on Sundays, as the Reading Quaker, Thomas Ellwood, soon discovered when he galloped off in the direction of Chalfont St Giles in Buckinghamshire – via Maidenhead – in order to attend a Religious Society of Friends meeting there in 1660, only to be arrested in Maidenhead where he was thrown into gaol for daring to ride his horse on the Sabbath. After much argument – protesting, to the astonishment of his gaolers, that he did not believe that it was against God's law to ride horses on Sundays – Ellwood was sufficiently persuasive (or his gaolers were sufficiently tolerant) to get himself released after several hours when he was allowed to resume his journey to Chalfont St Giles, where he arrived presumably too late for his meeting. A very enlightened and forward-thinking Christian sect, the Quakers suffered persecution in Britain, which is why the Englishman William Penn joined a great many of them in the US in 1682 to establish a colony there that then became Pennsylvania (where there is a town called Reading). They rejected the use of titles, religious oaths and holy sacraments, while also refusing to call other men 'sir', as was the custom in Britain. They believed in their 'inner light' and that God was grossly misrepresented by Protestants and Catholics.

Maidenhead Bridge across the River Thames is also said to have been the meeting place for a number of grandees, including Warren Hastings, the Viceroy of India in the early days of the Raj, and the town was once notable as an overnight resting place for horse-drawn coaches journeying to and from London at the rate of some 90 coaches a day, which was a lot of noisy traffic by any standard. So we can see that Maidenhead was a very busy, popular and prosperous little town in the days of its infancy (prosperous, that is, for the merchant classes and those who dealt with them).

Warren Hastings was England's colonial administrator in India in 1774 – England's first governor general there – and it is more or less generally agreed that his was an outstanding administration. On a return visit to London he arranged to meet his wife on Maidenhead Bridge, who came all the way from Cheltenham in Gloucester to meet him there. They almost certainly would have booked into the best inn around at that time – the first-class Orkney Arms at the side of Maidenhead Bridge that later became the luxury Skindle's Hotel (that is, alas, no more) mentioned previously in this chapter. Since Hastings's wife was holidaying at Cheltenham Spa at the time, she had a long journey to make on 13 June 1783 in order to meet up with her famous husband.

On another occasion, the Duke of Clarence – the future William IV – is supposed to have summoned his mistress to Maidenhead Bridge, the Irish stage actress Mrs Dorothy Jordan, also all the way from Cheltenham, simply to tell her that their relationship was over. She was starring in a play at the Cheltenham Theatre entitled *The Devil to Pay*. Given that the Duke had 10 children by her – how she found time to act as well is quite mystifying – it is hard to understand how he could possibly have dismissed her, just like that, back in the 18th century.

Mrs Jordan was a great success as a comic actress, not least for her brilliant performance, by all accounts, in *The Country Girl* (about which, presumably, this country girl knew a great deal as the mistress of a Duke and a future king, and 10 children to prove it!) The Duke of Clarence didn't get to be king until he was in his 60s. He was a Hanoverian known as 'Sailor Bill', having served in the Royal Navy as an admiral and acquired in consequence a taste for what was politely called 'naval language'. We are told by his biographers that he was 'surrounded by a numerous progeny of bastards', and that he had a theatrical and burlesque character, and, certainly, to summon the mother of his children all the way from Cheltenham to Maidenhead Bridge so that he could dismiss her there sounds very theatrical indeed!

But, not all members of royalty came to Maidenhead to do dirty deeds or to play pranks on the priesthood. Later on in history, George III and his family also visited the town to enjoy a day out at the horse races, and, as is very likely, the highwayman Dick Turpin may have attended to enjoy a good night out robbing horse-drawn coaches! George III was the mad, early 19th-century king, who allegedly attempted to influence parliament through corrupt 'king's friends' – cash for questions – and he was blamed for the loss of the American colonies. At the same time, his reign was responsible for the eventual victory over France in the Napoleonic Wars (thanks chiefly to Nelson and the Duke of Wellington), and for the introduction of Britain's agricultural and early Industrial Revolution (thanks, no doubt, to prime minister Pitt the Younger). The madness from which the king suffered has been attributed to the metabolic disease acute intermittent porphyria, which led to his becoming permanently insane, but it is nice to think of the poor man having some nice days out with his family at the Maidenhead races, and indeed of agricultural Maidenhead, Berkshire and the Thames Valley generally benefitting from the agricultural and early industrial Revolution reforms of his reign.

King William of Orange's soldiers came to Maidenhead in the late 17th century when the town welcomed him and his new constitutional monarchy in preference to monarchies inspired by a Divine Right of Kings to rule as they wished with the blessing of the church (and more particularly the Vatican). Irish Catholic troops opposing William of Orange fled over Maidenhead Bridge before the new king arrived from Holland. It was he who defeated the Irish Catholic in Ireland at the Battle of the Boyne, still celebrated to this day by Irish Protestants in Ulster. A lot of Catholics still argue that the only reason the English wanted out of the Catholic Church was because Henry VIII insisted upon it in order to have as many wives as he pleased – yet he still died a Catholic – but there is much more to it than that. Most of the English had had more than enough of a Catholic-inspired Divine Right of Kings, not to mention an interfering and bullying priesthood that could not have been less interested in democracy and constitutional government if it tried, especially the Catholics in those days. When William of Orange came to power, laws were passed to prevent Catholics ever again becoming monarchs or marrying monarchs in the United Kingdom.

What a thing it would be for the people of Maidenhead today to have a Heritage History Festival, with all these characters from the pages of history in period dress parading down the high street and along the river banks: the Vicar of Bray; the Duke of Clarence, his mistress and their children; Oliver Cromwell and Charles I with his children before he was beheaded; the great Brunel, who built Maidenhead's railway bridge over the river; Sir

Robert Taylor, who built the stone bridge that replaced the wooden bridge across the river; Dick Turpin, who very likely robbed people at Maidenhead Thicket; George III and his family gambling at Maidenhead Racecourse; Warren Hastings and his wife meeting on Maidenhead Bridge from the days of the Raj; and goodness knows how many others who have made history in the town – not to mention those people from the 1960s Profumo sex and spy scandal at nearby Cliveden – all disporting themselves and saying how do to passers by! King Alfred the Great – Berkshire's bravest and best son – who put an end to Danish Viking dominance in England and saved the country from Danish rule, could join the procession, as could Julius Caesar, who also came to Maidenhead with his troops, as could William the Conqueror with his Norman invaders, who built the castle at nearby Windsor, as could Queen Elizabeth I, who granted the status of township to Maidenhead and held court at nearby Bisham Abbey. And let's not forget the 'Cliveden Set' that held its secret meetings at nearby Cliveden to see if it couldn't persuade the British government to do a deal with Hitler, or Stirling Moss who drove the racing car – the Vanwall, built in Maidenhead – that became the first British car to win a British Grand Prix since 1934, or the pilots of the world's first vertical take-off airliner (the Fairey Rotodyne), the first flight of which was in Maidenhead.

All the materials of history are available to local historians and others to make a great spectacle for the enjoyment and enlightenment of townspeople and their children. It's just a matter of realising the potential of these materials and using them to good effect.

Without doubt, Maidenhead really could do with a sense of its own history. There are few independently published history books about the town – not including picture books, self-published booklets, books about certain aspects of local history or books that take a look at not more than a few centuries in the overall history of the town – and Maidenhead doesn't even have a museum that writers of local history can go to when researching their books, or that history students and their teachers, or members of the public for that matter, can visit. At the time of writing (November 2006), the little art museum at neighbouring Cookham for the works of the English artist the late Sir Stanley Spencer is closed for refurbishment, and Spencer's paintings have had to go all the way to the Reading museum for safe keeping and exhibition.

We are told by J. Wesley Walker, in his aforementioned 1930s *History of Maidenhead*, that there was a museum in the town that was temporarily housed in Maidenhead's newly-opened Lending Library in 1904, which came complete with a Librarian's House (mein got!) but with nothing more than some temporary, makeshift space for a museum, along with the library's reading and magazine rooms, lending, references and store rooms. So the museum was the poor relation of the library (which sounds like a very odd arrangement). At some point later on it seems to have disappeared without trace – a strange way of managing the town's priorities and, indeed, honouring its history.

Reading, by contrast, has had a proper museum from the word go that still exists to this day (where I spent many a happy hour as a child back in the 1950s).

Why Maidenhead has neglected its history in this way is hard to understand, and if any readers have further information about this I am all ears. It is not clear when or why Maidenhead's early 20th-century temporary museum ceased to exist, or never really got off the ground in the first place, but it does seem peculiar that Maidenhead never seriously bothered with a proper museum. To have a permanent sense of its own history – or even of history generally – a town cannot make do with a temporary museum or no museum at all. No wonder historical artefacts and other remains have gone elsewhere, to other places that have taken care to have museums of their own.

What there is now in Maidenhead in the new millennium is a recently peripatetic Heritage Centre – without a home for more than a decade since its foundation in the 1990s – that has been in search of a permanent spot in the town for which it has, to its credit, raised £1 million, with which it has recently bought the freehold of an old and derelict pub called the Cricketers Arms in Maidenhead's Park Street in the centre of town.

This pub – which one hopes is not too little too late – is two minutes' walk from Maidenhead Library and high street, located behind the old town hall, with on-street parking immediately outside its entrance. It sounds (and looks) like a rum place for a museum – lacking the gravitas and indeed the dignity of such buildings – but I guess it's got to be better than nothing. I suppose that beggars can't be choosers, so well done Heritage Centre volunteers. The centre has a website and organises talks and lectures for interested parties, including schools and clubs, and it is making a very spirited attempt to bring history alive in the town, but it has not as yet managed to turn itself into a proper museum with all the proper facilities.

At the time of writing, the centre is located at number 3 Kingsway in King Street, Maidenhead, near the New Market, and close to the Methodist Church. It is certainly making a valiant attempt to put local history on the map, and it presumably has many more stories about Maidenhead's local history than I have included in this chapter, but who in the community knows about these stories, other than the relative few at the Heritage Centre and the small number of people who attend its talks?

These stories and the history of Maidenhead need to be projected to a much wider public, with the help of the local and perhaps even the national media and of regional television, if the history of this town is to be brought fully alive and restored to its proper place.

The only possible interest in the above gossipy little stories about Maidenhead Bridge is that they show what a fashionable and truly-national landmark it had become early on in its history – in contrast to today – with a once-upon-a-time mystique and romance all its own that had captured the imagination of the nation and also of imperialists as far away as British India in the days of the Raj, who would have spoken of meeting on Maidenhead Bridge when they got back to the UK, where the bridge was firmly in place in the national consciousness.

Never dismiss the trivia of history because it can often help us understand the lager picture, not least in a town like Maidenhead where the larger picture may not at first appear all that large – at least on the face of it.

We are reminded by these little stories of how times and places change in the fullness of time. Whoever thinks of Maidenhead Bridge today? But there was a time when people of substance who ventured outside the capital city of London, in search of somewhere to meet, immediately thought of nearby Maidenhead Bridge, and not of the less accessible bridges (by road) at Windsor, Marlow or Henley, because it was much easier to get to, on a direct east–west route, and at this time in its history it had all the hostelry to go with it.

But if it had upmarket hostelry for the Warren Hastings of this world, at the same time it also had downmarket hostelry for Irish agricultural and other labourers. For example, they would come to England in search of employment, travelling in their carts and wagons, and staying either at the downmarket Criterion lodging house (to the rear of 100 Maidenhead High Street today) or with the legendary Mother Greengrass at Boyne Hill, by all accounts a fiery woman with a rough tongue as sharp as a bacon slicer and a colourful vocabulary to go with it. According to folklore, when she was behind with her rent and a young bailiff was sent like a strutting turkeycock to relieve her of one of her pigs to clear her arrears, she threw a bucket of hot water over his head as he bent down to take her pig, scalding his face and whiskers!

All this was long before the arrival of the railways in Maidenhead, a century before World War Two, when Maidenhead Station became the first and last stop for trains travelling to and from London (there was no station at Slough, which was a sleepy village at the time – nothing like the trading estate it became later). The new station came with a new railway bridge across the river by the famous engineer Isambard Brunel, after whom Brunel University was named and whose masterpiece became the largest brickwork construction in the country. It was quickly immortalised by the equally-famous painter William Turner – one of the greatest English painters of all time – whose painting of Maidenhead Bridge remains a classic to this day (see chapter nine).

Added to these intriguing, lesser-known facts is the ownership of Maidenhead's first coaching inn by a 15th-century female business entrepreneur – some two centuries ahead of other female entrepreneurs – not to mention, in more recent times, the aforesaid 1950s Vanwall racing car and the first flight of the world's first vertical take-off airliner.

As I say, quite a startling little history.

So many historical figures have passed through and stayed in Maidenhead in their time, bringing a flood of colourful glimpses from the outside world into this small country town to broaden its mind and provide it with food for thought. There were grandees and MPs from London, including several monarchs; a mightily-famous engineer and an equally-famous artist both from London; governors and doubtless others besides from far-away British India; notable people from Cheltenham Spa at a time in English history when that city was highly fashionable and too far away for most of the locals to go there; a 15th-century female entrepreneur ahead of her time running an inn; Ancient Britons, Romans, Irish agricultural and other labourers, Danish Vikings, Norman French and Germanic Anglo-Saxons who chased away the Ancient Britons, most of whom came to Maidenhead.

As we can see from the above – and this is a matter that has not been fully explored in previous local histories of Maidenhead or Berkshire – far from being the proud, strictly Anglo-Saxon community that, in common with other English and Berkshire towns, Maidenhead has always fancied itself as, the town has been much more pan-European than is generally realised, with an overriding DNA out of Rome, France and Denmark, as well as out of Saxony. Throughout its history, Maidenhead has been a community sometimes cast in a Saxon and other times in a Norman mould, until, in the final processes of its and the nation's history, it cast itself in a truly English mould. So most of the place names are Saxon, but that is only because the Saxons took care to change the names that went before – the place names from the Romans and the Ancient Britons – and they made sure to cast themselves in an English mould by laying down the law to the Danish invaders and obliging them, if they wanted to stay on in England – which a great many of them did – to stop messing about and to tow the line and obey the law, and to stop pillaging, raping and pushing the locals around.

Although most people in Maidenhead today would almost certainly tell you that they are of Anglo-Saxon stock if you stopped and asked them on the street, the chances are that they may not, in fact, be cast quite as much in the Anglo-Saxon English mould as they believe.

But what, one might ask, is a truly English mould?

Don't all answer at once!

It is, of course, cultural and social rather than racial – an emotion and a state of mind – and it seems to me that it is the colour of one's culture and emotions rather than one's skin that makes for the most important difference of all.

As I know from my own upbringing and life experiences in Berkshire and the Thames Valley, the whole region is 'proud to be English' and quite right too, because it is typically English in so many important ways, and 'Royal Berkshire' after all. What else can it be other than Anglo-Saxon English? But this does not alter the fact that this typical Englishness came from some very untypical racial and historical processes, with Roman, Danish, Germanic Anglo-Saxon and French antecedents. So how Anglo-Saxon is that? As in other parts of the country, Maidenhead's and Berkshire's English folk have come out of an inter-racial melting pot from the very beginning. Yet you would not think so, travelling through their typically-English countryside, much of which is picture-postcard country with English cottages and pastoral scenes everywhere in evidence.

As for my Berkshire parents, who were not big on genealogy and had no interest in family trees, they considered themselves English and were proud to be so, to which I reply, yes, be proud to be English and preserve your culture and traditions, but don't shut out the outside world (not that England ever has; it has a better cosmopolitan record than most) since that is where your ancestors came from and went to. They came out of Europe, and they went to the four corners of the earth, not least to the United States, Canada, Australia and South Africa, and into the Asian continent of India, where they bred with the natives and gave rise to a new breed of British Eurasians (called Anglo-Indians today). A Saxon Warrior King called Taeppa is buried outside Maidenhead in nearby Taplow, and it is quite true that a Saxon parliament once met at nearby Cookham, and that King Alfred the Great was a Wantage-born Berkshire man who saved England from the Danes, but that doesn't rule out all the other races that have been in and around Maidenhead, and let's not forget that Roman Villa at Cox Green or the original inhabitants of Cookham who were Ancient Britons and Romans.

This is only my point of view, but what is the point of studying history unless you use your logical deduction in order to arrive at a point of view, and it has always seemed to me that this is the inescapable racial message that those who keep their wits about them must surely learn from local history when delving into the past of so many towns like Maidenhead. This is the international context that we come to understand from digging into our local and national histories.

But there were – I hear you say – Ancient Britons in and around Maidenhead before the Anglo-Saxons arrived on the scene out of Saxon Europe, and that is perfectly true. But the chances are that these Ancient Britons came out of Europe also, as we shall see from the following chapter.

———————————————————

CHAPTER TWO

The Earth History
of Maidenhead

The history of Maidenhead earth and stone is longer than the life-and-times history of the people who have lived in the town from one generation to the next, and it is a history that has happened and been recorded in earth and stone – just as the people's history has happened in life itself and been written in manuscripts, records and books – which is why we must study the ground for a different kind of historical knowledge, not of the known people and the known events but of what went before.

And when we do this, we soon discover that the ground and the soil itself are whispering to us of unknown and ill-defined prehistoric people who existed before the known, clearly-defined and documented people who came later on.

Maidenhead's earth history – which is Berkshire's earth history – tells us that Berkshire and the places where Maidenhead began (Bray, Cookham, Pinkney's Green, Elentone and South Ellington) started life as an old sea bed, not as old as the hills, as the saying goes, but older than the hills – as old as the sea itself.

We know from this amazing earth history that ancient sea shells have been discovered in different parts of Berkshire, suggesting that the entire county really was a great seabed that turned, in time, to chalk, which over centuries – and with millions and millions of shells – eventually made the chalky Berkshire hills, known as the Berkshire Downs, through which the River Thames (the German Rhine originally) found its way through what we call the Thames Valley today, and then through the area that became the town of Maidenhead as a result of this river.

Without the earth and the river developing in the way in which it did from the beginning of time, there would be no people history of Maidenhead or elsewhere in Britain. So were we lucky to inherit the earth and the rivers that we inherited? Compared with other parts of the world, of course we were.

We also know, from massive beds of oyster shells deep down in the Berkshire clay, that this seabed-county became a great estuary, like the Thames Estuary today on the eastern side of London (we know this because oysters have made a habit of making their homes in estuaries).

It is from all this that we can see yesterday's seas covered what became today's earth, today's earth that may very well become – with the long and heavy tread of time and history – tomorrow's sea in a great circular motion. Having brought the land into being in the first place, the sea may wash it all away again!

With this in mind, we can understand how the geographical stage (a chalky stage in this part of the country) was set for the history of Maidenhead and the whole of Berkshire to commence, and we can also see the magical connection between Maidenhead – that is far indeed from the seaside – and the sea around Britain's shores, not that most people today would make such a connection; on the contrary, they would automatically think of Maidenhead as an inland riverside and not a seaside town.

But when we look into earth history, we can see that Maidenhead and all of Berkshire's landscape rose up out of the sea by the force of nature, before any human being laid a hand on it.

In order to know this for sure, we look into the chalky Berkshire earth, with all its rolling hills, to discover another geophysical and geographical history written there, not only in the chalk but in the clay at Oxford and Reading and in the gravel and sand ridges in different parts of the county. We look into a landscape that is positively bristling with a very different history of its own, a history of flint and stone in which there is no coal to be found in the ground (other than some very scanty trace elements) as there was and is in other parts of the UK, and the reason there is no coal in Maidenhead and Berkshire ground is because coal, being the residue in the long passage of time of forests that have sunk below the sea, is not to be found in sea beds that have turned themselves into a positive ooze of chalk (along with some gravel, sand and clay in different places).

Tell the people of Maidenhead today that the ground of their most ancient forbears in Berkshire towns and villages has risen up out of a sea bed, and they will look at you askance, because they, their parents and grandparents have all grown up in the knowledge that they are inland river people, not coastal or seaside people. But then explain to them about the chalk and its origins and see if that doesn't open their eyes wide and capture their imaginations!

What a subject for regional television in Berkshire and the Thames Valley this would be, but who are the local history editors there? There are none. These television channels are as far removed from local history as men on the moon, as are the local radio stations.

Because the sand and gravel that covers the chalk in different parts of Berkshire – where the earth is less fertile as a result – is barren and flat, it makes for excellent sporting facilities, golf courses and horse-racing tracks, and, as we know, the Royal Ascot racecourse is not too far from Maidenhead, as is the Newbury racecourse, and we have also seen how in the 18th and 19th centuries Maidenhead had a racecourse of its own that was attended by royals, as Ascot still is today, as already mentioned in the previous chapter.

According to *Companion into Berkshire*, in 1787 'George III and all his family attended the horse races there [Maidenhead]'. The same publication also tells us that 'three gentlemen' were held up and robbed by a single highwayman 'with a black mask in Maidenhead thicket'. Thousands of years after Maidenhead's earth history with its scary cavemen, some scary highwaymen were behaving as before!

According to Wesley Walker, there were two racecourses in the town at different locations. He reckons that there was one on the south side of Altwood Road (where I had occasion to live in the 1960s and I have relatives living near this road currently), where there was a great chunk of land between Tittle Row and Cox Green, and from Boyne Hill to Canon Chalk Pit that adjoined Maidenhead Thicket, and then another between Camly Corner and Waltham Siding, where a horse owned by a Mr John Higgs beat another owned by the proprietor of the Sun Inn (Mr Tagg). But this author does not tell us why Maidenhead's famous racecourse ceased to be. All he says about it is that it was 'quite an important function' in the local and royal 'social calendar' once upon a time, when it was 'patronised by royalty', but that it was discontinued round 'about 1815'.

But if the sand and gravel earth has been good for horse racing and golf in Maidenhead and other parts of Berkshire, there is also the aforesaid clay in the county – at Reading just down the road from Maidenhead and at Oxford at the other inland end of the Thames Valley – and there is clay again in London at the eastern end of the valley. There have also been brickfields at Slough and Bracknell from which the capital city of London and the capital town of Berkshire (Reading) were built at a rapid rate, as indeed was Maidenhead when the time came.

The geophysical and geographical stage that the earth history has set for the commencement of the people history in Berkshire and Maidenhead was set for flint and stone-age men, and for wild beasts also, and the flint tools of the former are everywhere in evidence in the Thames Valley, and not least in the Reading and Newbury museums. There are also the remains of cracked and splintered animal bones that show how flesh was hacked from them in the massively distant past, so that meat could be taken and presumably eaten raw, because there is no apparent evidence of fire in the caves, peat dwellings or wooden huts, where these frightfully early men and women lived (always on the move in search of animals they could hunt in order to feed themselves, presumably dressing in their skins).

These were the Ancient Britons, who existed before the Romans and Anglo-Saxons arrived on the scene, and, predictably, they would have been out-and-out savages whose brutal existence had turned them into hunter gatherers, hunting ox, deer, horses and other beasts, including mammoths. We have learnt this from the remains at our disposal at the Victoria and Albert Museum in London.

These flesh-eating hunter gatherers were to be found in and around the swampy territory of the early river Thames up and down the Berkshire valley. They must have been hairy, hardy men, in those primitive times before electric razors and aftershave, who would make your hair stand on end if you had the dubious pleasure of encountering them today!

They came out of darkest Berkshire – darkest Britannia – in the same way that tribal savages have come out of darkest Africa in their time, and, in due course, they managed to graduate from being hunters to settled herdsmen and tillers of soil, living in settled rather than nomadic communities, which is how the largely agricultural and rural community of Maidenhead and Berkshire got started, with all its farms and agricultural produce.

Tell the people of Maidenhead and Berkshire today that their ancestors came out of a Western equivalent of Darkest Africa – living in caves and also underground in dug outs rather than up trees – but that they had climate on their side to set about civilising themselves as and when the spirit moved them, and see how they react? Tell them that these early people had to look abroad to learn the rudimentary arts of civilisation – to Rome and to what is Belgium today (as we shall see later on in this chapter) – and they will very likely look askance yet again. On the other hand, those that do not look askance will perhaps grasp the significance of this and have a quite different attitude to the dark regions of the outside world, including Africa, and understand the difference that this knowledge of their own darkest local history makes to them in the world view that they take today.

The first Berkshire village is reckoned to have been at Coxwell, near Farringdon, where deep holes were dug in sandy and gravely soil at a place known as Coles Pits, which is where the first-known Berkshire tribe appears to have settled, up in the Berkshire Downs near Ashbury, more than 3,000 years ago, where a cave known as Wayland Smiths Cave is claimed to be the oldest in the county. Because Wayland Smiths Cave was furnished with heavy stone that could not have been carried or built without the collective communal efforts of an entire tribe of people – who put a tomb inside their cave for their chieftain – then it seems safe to assume that there was a settled tribe here that lived, worked and pulled their weight together as a community, the first-known tribe in Berkshire.

When the first Germanic Anglo-Saxons turned up in the Thames Valley, they gave this settlement the name of Wayland Smiths Cave, and they did what all tribes have done all over the world from the beginning of time: they spun a mythology around it and the things they did not understand about it, having named it after their own mythological Saxon smith-god Wayland

Smith, and they also drove out the descendants of Berkshire's first settled tribes.

This has always been the way of the world, and we should not forget it. Nor should we dismiss mythology in our study of history because, though far from factual, much of the time it clearly demonstrates how people tried to make sense of what they did not understand, which was as incomprehensible to them at that time as they are to us today (relatively speaking).

This Anglo-Saxon smith-god, after whom the remains of Berkshire's first village has been named, was supposed to have married a Swan Maiden called Hervor, and there is also a burial mound in Oxfordshire known as Wayland's Smithy (presumably where there was a workshop for blacksmiths and other smiths).

Where these early Ancient Britons, who first settled in and around Maidenhead and the wider Thames Valley, came from in the first place – before the Saxons showed their faces on the scene – is anybody's guess, but the chances are that they came from the east along the line of the Thames at Maidenhead and elsewhere (as did the Romans who followed in due course) from what we now know as London, and that they either arrived by marching or riding (let's not forget those horses remains) across the North Sea, which was dry land at that time, or by coming across the English Channel in boats from Belgium, where there were other tribes and communities on the look out for pastures new. It does not seem likely that they could have come from anywhere else, so again we see how we all seem to have come out of Europe, including these Ancient Britons, and not just from North Sea Europe but from parts southwards across the English Channel that later became known as Belgian and French Europe.

For more information about the Ancient Britons, readers would do well to refer to the writings of the early Romans who came to England and fought the natives, but such writings are beyond the scope of this book.

Suffice it to say that it is generally agreed that the first person to have written an account of Berkshire and its Ancient Britons was Julius Caesar in 55BC when he arrived in the Thames Valley – via Kent, his first port of call – crossing the River Thames with his troops at a location that later became the village and then the town of Maidenhead in the fullness of time. We are told by the 16th-century scholar and antiquarian William Camden in *Britannia* that he supposes that Bray was 'occupied by the Bibroci who submitted to Caesar, and I have good grounds for such a supposition…Bibracle in France is now contracted into [the name of] Bray, and not far from this place Caesar crossed the Thames with his army where these people submitted to him. Among these Bibroci stands Windsor, called by the Saxons, perhaps by the windings of the [river] bank.' (William Camden's *Britannia* is a very important source for researching local and national history, as we shall see in the following chapter.)

So these Ancient Britons – like the Normans later on (although they were of Danish origin) – came out of France and Belgium, and we know from Julius Caesar that they had cattle, horses and war chariots and were a formidable foe. Caesar came to subdue them because they had been assisting the Belgian tribes of Gaul (from whom, remember, the Ancient Brits may have descended) in their war against the Romans. It was from the Belgian Gauls and, subsequently, the Romans that the Ancient Britons learnt some of the rudimentary arts of civilisation, although they had already civilised themselves to some extent by herding cattle, cultivating land and trading with the Gaul.

Again we see the importance of making international connections with local history. Only by doing so can we understand where our civilisation comes from and how it is arrived at. In Maidenhead and Berkshire the international connections – evidenced by local history – teach us the following:

(1) That most races, including the British and the people of Maidenhead, have, of course, come out of their own darkest Africa (darkest Africa is still with us today, but all races have been there).

(2) The very first people to have settled in what we know as Maidenhead and Berkshire today were originally from tribes located in Continental Europe at places that we know as Belgium and France, to whom they were indebted for their very first civilising influences, to be indebted thereafter to the Romans, by whom they were enslaved and civilised into the bargain.

(3) What the Anglo-Saxon ancestors of the people of Maidenhead and Berkshire had in common with the Ancient Greeks and Israelites is that they spun a mythology (at Wayland's Cave) about the things they did not understand (albeit not with the same colourful imaginations or universal success!).

(4) The blood of some of the ancestors of today's people of Maidenhead and Berkshire – together with people from other parts of the UK – was scattered around Europe and the Middle East by the Romans, when they enslaved the best of the Ancient Briton warrior class and sent them off to fight in different parts of their empire, where it is inconceivable that they did not mate with women of other races and leave Ancient British blood in those places. It is also inconceivable that Romans did not interbreed with Ancient Britons, in which case there is Roman blood in Ancient British veins.

There was a Roman ruler called Agricola – whose father-in-law was the great Tacitus – who ruled out of Silchester on the southern borders of Berkshire, south of Reading – a village in which Roman remains have been found, including the site of an arena and an amphitheatre.

The Romans built roads and garrison towns all over Berkshire as well as villas, including a villa at Castle Hill, Maidenhead, and just as the British came and went from India in the days of the Raj, civilising and exploiting that country, so the Romans came and went from Britain and Berkshire, civilising and exploiting those places, taking care to enslave the best of the British warriors and, as mentioned already, sending them off to Italy to serve in Roman armies in different parts of the Roman Empire – just as the British recruited Indian and other native tribesmen to serve in the armies of the British Empire.

In the absence of their best warriors, the Ancient Britons were easily pacified and had no choice but to become more peaceful and unwarlike – a pushover, in fact, for the Germanic Anglo-Saxons when they arrived – and when the Romans left Britain in 410 they looked for their last time on Berkshire and the Thames Valley as they marched down to the English coast and sailed back to Rome in their boats, leaving the denuded communities of the Ancient Britons free at last but defenceless when the Anglo-Saxons arrived.

Had they not been so, things might have turned out very differently indeed for England and its Anglo-Saxon roots, for the Ancient Britons were ferocious indeed. The Anglo-Saxons have the Romans to thank for clearing a path for them that was by no means uphill.

What we can say of Berkshire's Ancient Brits is that while their primary business was that of war we also know from sickles found at Bray (the so-called mother of Maidenhead) that there were some peaceful and more constructive pursuits in progress. What are curved-bladed sickles for, if not for the cutting of corn? We can also say that these Ancient Britons underwent a tremendous character and culture change as a result of the Roman occupation, and that they were soon to disappear completely with the arrival of the Anglo-Saxons. So there are few in Maidenhead and Berkshire today who can claim any lineage with the Ancient Britons who went elsewhere, to Wales and Ireland maybe, except for those who went all over the Roman Empire as warrior slaves. On the other hand, others may have remained and inter-bred with Saxons.

It is to the Anglo-Saxons – and maybe to some mixed-race Romans and Ancient Britons – that Thames Valley people can trace their lineage today, as well as to the Danish Vikings and Normans out of France. There were plenty of Normans in and around Windsor, including Maidenhead of course, on account of William the Conqueror building his Norman castle and establishing his court there with all his Norman lords, who would have been extremely unpopular with the local Anglo-Saxons. For this reason there are French-Norman names in these parts. So Maidenhead, throughout its history, has seen a Norman-French court and government at nearby Windsor, Anglo-Saxon courts and governments at nearby Taplow and Cookham – and also at Wantage up in the Berkshire Downs (as we shall see) – and Roman rule once upon a time (as well as the temporary Elizabethan court during the summer months at nearby Bisham Abbey).

Out of the earth history of Maidenhead and Berkshire, people have evolved in the way that they have, with their rulers and their courts, and they have come from early pre-historic times when the Thames Valley was inhabited by Palaeolithic Man from the time of the Ice Age, hunting along the banks of the Thames and extracting gravel from pits upstream from Maidenhead.

The animal remains mentioned previously, that have been found from this period, include those of horses, cow-like aurochs and the aforementioned hairy-coated mammoth elephants, with their curved tusks, and even rhinoceroses with their two-horned noses. It was following the Ice Age that the woods and forests began to flourish in the Thames Valley and human habitation reared its head, with both picks and axed-hammers unearthed in the ground. Canoes as well as Stone Age and Bronze Age implements have also been found, as have amber broaches and glass beads, and the oldest object in the collection of the Maidenhead Heritage Centre is reckoned to be some 4,000 years old.

What a fascinating and revealing subject geography is, and where would local history be without it?

But all this was long before the town of Maidenhead got started, and we shall come to that in the following chapter, when we take a great leap forward from ancient times, as we see what a complicated subject history is, and how useful it is if we are to truly understand how we have all come about and what we are about.

CHAPTER THREE

How Maidenhead Got Started

As has already been noted, Maidenhead got started as a small community that was half in the parishes of both Bray and Cookham, and, although it had a thriving little corporate life by reason of the foundation of the Guild of St Andrew and St Mary Magdalen in 1451, it wasn't until the town was incorporated by a royal charter of Queen Elizabeth I in 1582 that it seriously got going.

Even as late at 1821, only 950 people lived in the town, but when the railways came in 1841 its population rocketed to 3,315. In the new millennium, the population of Maidenhead at the last count was 59,605.

From 950 to 59,605 people in 186 years is not such a great population explosion. However, it is steady enough, and without the coming of the railways to Maidenhead this growth would have been far slower, and Maidenhead may very well have returned to the village that it once was, as the horse-drawn carriages ceased to stop over in the town in the new railway age that followed.

No doubt some of the stories in the first chapter about Mrs Greengrass's Irish guests – and about the Duke of Clarence and Mrs Jordan – have been embroidered a little or a lot, but it doesn't alter the fact that these people were coming to Maidenhead once upon a time, contributing to the development of the town and spending their money.

What matters is that Irish labourers did stay with Mrs Greengrass, not whether she did or did not throw a bucket of hot water over a bailiff's head, as, by all accounts, she did. What matters overall is that the said meetings did take place on Maidenhead Bridge and in its coaching inns, not whether or not people did what they are supposed to have done when they met there.

Maybe some of the 1960s stories about the Profumo Affair sex and spy scandals at nearby Cliveden were embroidered, but it doesn't alter the fact that the events in question happened alright, as we know from recent history, and with so much talk about highwaymen and robbers hiding out at Maidenhead Thicket in the days of highwaymen and robbers throughout the Thames Valley and the rest of the country, it is not logical to suppose that many of these stories are likely to have been invented. Some may have been, but not most.

Perhaps the James I and Vicar of Bray story may or may not have been embroidered and invented, but the point is that English monarchs have been coming to Maidenhead to hunt, as we also know from Wesley Walker who tells us in his book that the royal hounds were hunted 'for some years' in Maidenhead before eventually being handed over to the Berks and Bucks Farmers Staghounds. The royal pack was discontinued in 1901.

Put all of this borderline history together – the history of fact, fancy and apocryphalia – and you have a very good feel for different states of mind and the community spirit of the times, and any history that ignores states of mind and community spirit also ignores how people were feeling and what they were worrying and gossiping about.

Which brings us to the seriously factual story of Maidenhead and how it got started with its wooden bridge over the Thames and its elusive maiden. The bridge served its purpose and so, too, did the maiden, albeit in a less tangible but more symbolic way in the case of the latter.

Without the bridge there would have been no Maidenhead, and without the image of a maiden there would have been no such place name.

Never mind about splitting hairs over the contradictory origins and meanings of the word 'maiden', and whether or not it was actually intended to refer to a virginal maiden at all (as may not have been the case) because the fact is that a maiden is what the people of Maidenhead got, intentionally or otherwise, and they were generally pleased to have her because they could easily have changed the place name of their town had they not warmed to their maiden. The people of Maidenhead like the idea of a maiden!

The point – laboured by some previous local historians – is not whether the town was actually intended to be named after a maiden or whether its name came to it by default, but that Maidenhead is what the town was called, mistakenly or otherwise, and what an excellent name it is – so where's the problem?

We know that Maidenhead in Berkshire is one of several riverside towns in the Thames Valley west of London, some 28 miles from London's Hyde Park Corner – approximately 50 miles by river from London Bridge and 24 miles by train from Paddington Station in the West of London – having come into existence as a town in 1582 when Queen Elizabeth I conferred the status of township upon it, granting this Thameside settlement a licence to have its own mayor and town corporation, as well as some Elizabethan street fairs and farmers' markets.

Mayors were called wardens in those days and you couldn't have a town until you were incorporated by a monarch with the appointment of a warden. This new town had previously existed as a hamlet centuries before the Elizabethan age. This was when Danish Vikings reportedly sailed up the Thames in the ninth century, disembarking at a place that became known to history as South Ellenton, Aylington, Ealington or Ellington (I shall use the latter version in this book), and the reason why the Danes disembarked there was to prepare themselves for a war against Reading, which was the conquering invaders next port of call.

But it was in Reading where things eventually began to go wrong for the Vikings, because the Anglo-Saxon King Alfred the Great came down from the Berkshire Downs – he was born in Wantage – and went in disguise among the enemy on the streets of Reading after the Danes had taken the town, spying on them and preparing to drive them out of his kingdom, which he managed to do after waging a protracted guerrilla war. They slogged it out with the Danes and eventually fought them to an absolute standstill before taking London back from Danish rule and restoring the capital city to the Anglo-Saxon English, of which Alfred was proud to be king. King Alfred's soldiers came initially from Maidenhead, Windsor, Reading and from throughout Berkshire, Buckinghamshire, Oxfordshire, Hampshire, Wiltshire, Somerset and maybe also Dorset. While they were putting paid to the Danes in Alfred's kingdom and elsewhere – including

Kent and Exeter – the East Anglian English in the Norfolk/Suffolk kingdom of Mercier were also fighting them tooth and nail.

In due course, Berkshire became known as King Alfred the Great's own county and Reading became its capital city. After much fighting and bloodshed against the Danes, with deaths and defeats on both sides, King Alfred came to the throne of Wessex, decisively holding the balance of power and acknowledged as overlord of his own ever-expanding Kingdom of Wessex (which seems to have included Berkshire, the Upper Thames Basin up to the Cotswolds, Wiltshire, very probably Somerset and Dorset, and maybe even a tiny bit of South London at Southwark). As everybody knows, or thinks they know, Alfred was not only an outstanding warrior king but also a man of learning, administration and law, who did a lot to educate his people and run his kingdom justly. He also became the first English king to realise that it was better to fight an invader at sea before he reached the land than to stay put on land waiting for him to arrive. Having built himself a fleet of wooden ships, Alfred fought several battles against the Danes at sea and eventually sent them packing. He also sent the Sigehelm on a long and treacherous sea voyage to India to see if he could find the tomb of St Thomas (the connection with India goes way back, long before the Raj and the time when Warren Hastings came to Maidenhead Bridge to meet his wife there on a return visit to England). It is nothing less than mind-boggling to think of boats being sailed from England to India in the ninth century when the hazards and the challenges must have been awesome.

Having been brought up in the Berkshire Downs at Wantage, which was the home of the old Saxon kings and the capital of the county in those days, King Alfred the Great was, and remains, by far the greatest Berkshire man. Having based themselves in Reading, the Danish armies clashed with his Saxon armies somewhere near Ilsley and Compton, where a bloody battle raged, which the Danes lost. They were put to flight and pursued into Wiltshire, where they finally surrendered and signed a peace treaty, which allowed the Danish king to settle in the North of England and East Anglia (Mercia), where many of his fellow countrymen had already taken root, having plundered and seized villages, towns and estates there, and so it was King Alfred – the best and bravest of Berkshire's sons, as he has been called

– who saved the whole of Britain from Danish domination and rule. While the Danes were not expelled from the country, they had to know their place and toe the line from here on. No more pushing people around and trying to rule and tax them. They could stay in peace or go home, and a great many stayed in peace after King Alfred of Berkshire had managed to do what no other English chieftain or king had done, which was to give the Danes a bloody nose and put a stop to their warring once and for all. Predictably, Berkshire people who are aware of this history – as few are – are quite proud of the role that their ancestors played back in the mists of time in taming the Danes and releasing England from their bondage.

Today, hardy northerners in England regard themselves as the hard men of the country, not infrequently referring to people down south as 'nesh', 'soft southerners', 'southern Jessies' and 'a big girl's blouse'! But it was not forever thus – if it ever was at all – because it was the south that saved England from Danish domination, not the north, which didn't seem to be able to get its act or its defences together to stop the invading Vikings. While north country people became hard in the fullness of time – as a result of the extremely hard and harsh times to which they were exposed by the Industrial Revolution, the steel works and the coal mines – most southerners had an easier time of it. But back in the days of King Alfred the Great it was the gritty and hardy south that was showing its mettle.

Again we see the international and national connections, and the present-day importance of making these connections when studying local history, which are:

(1) It's not just that the English have plenty of Danish and Anglo-Saxon blood in their veins – out of Northern Europe – but that if it had not been for the Anglo-Saxons in Maidenhead, Reading, Berkshire and the then County of Wessex, the entire country, including London, would have come under Danish imperial rule, which was by no means a civilising, educating or religious rule but seems to have been a particularly nasty, barbaric and exploitative rule that would have put the clock back for English civilisation and culture. The Saxon kings were in Wessex and Berkshire, which was where the mobilising force and impetus came from to bring the Danish Viking reign of terror to an end and to restore London to the English. Of

course, the rest of the country joined the struggle against the Danes, but it was King Alfred and the men of Berkshire who were the heroes in the vanguard against the Danes, demonstrating as they did that the Danes could be beaten and driving them into defeat (ably assisted by East Anglia and other counties). The North of England was not as well organised as Berkshire and Wessex to protect itself against the Danes, and it was to the North of England that most of the Danes were banished by King Alfred the Great.

(2) The difference that this local history makes to national history today is that London would have become a Danish city architecturally and otherwise. The English would not have become as civilised or law-abiding as they did early on in their history – it would have taken longer under the savage Danes – and London may not have become the seat of English kings and queens (the Danes were especially powerful in York). Had the people of Berkshire, Maidenhead and Wessex not been on a relentless warpath against the Danish Vikings, England may never have been rid of them because the rest of England may not have rallied to the rousing war cries of the Berkshire and Wessex people, or been inspired by their successes.

(3) And without doubt, far-away India would not have been discovered as early as it was by Sighelm because King Alfred would not have been in a position to build ships and send him there.

(4) Equally, and without doubt, the English would not have taught themselves the military value of a navy, which is what Alfred the Great taught them when he built himself a fleet of ships to fight the Danes at sea (his father before him had also built ships).

(5) It is no exaggeration to say that it was Berkshire and Wessex people who originally put England and London on the map as a country and a city in its own right nationally and internationally. When the French-speaking Normans (also of Danish origin) came, the country was up and running thanks to Berkshire and its Saxon kings. It is hardly surprising that the English are so proud of their Anglo-Saxon origins, however accurate they may or may not be. These Saxons were a truly remarkable people who seldom, if at all, took no for an answer and who never took defeat lying down. On the contrary, they persisted until they had turned their losses

into success, and what a success they made of their country, out of the Berkshire / Wessex kingdom of Alfred the Great (although Berkshire joined with Wessex in the campaign against the Danes, it seems to have otherwise kept its own proud identity as a separate county, distinct from Wessex).

One of the reasons that this doesn't sink in with the people of Maidenhead anymore is because this is not how local history is taught in Berkshire and other parts of the country.

In the new millennium all this stuff about the Danes seems rather absurd and irrelevant, but back then one can well imagine how serious and important it was to those who did not want to pay the *Danegeld* anymore, to those who did not want to be pushed around by invaders from Denmark (or Normandy for that matter), and one can very easily see the difference that this slice of all-important history – getting shot of the Danes – has made to the way we all are in England today, to the character of an island race whose ancestors were not suited to the Danish character and were having none of it.

Looking at the peace-loving Danish character today, we do not see them as a martial race, so we can see how people and times change. Listening to today's Danes – who war on no one – one would think that butter wouldn't melt in their mouths, but it was not always so. They and their fellow Scandinavians and Norsemen were fearsome and shameless imperialists, once upon a time, and they would have made England their own if they could.

But how many people know this?

Only the few who know their history.

It is interesting to note that all of Berkshire's Saxon, Danish and Norman ancestors have met in war and settled in peace – as they have throughout England – leaving the Romans and the Ancient Britons to go elsewhere, but not without these latter people leaving their inescapable trace elements in English blood and in English history. The Romans lasted some 400 years in England, before leaving it defenceless and open to Anglo-Saxon and Danish invaders. Obviously, England was up for grabs in those days – even the Picts and the Scots had invaded from the north, so everybody was at it – after the Romans had made themselves scarce. But the Romans had left a civilised society behind them, not least in Berkshire and the South – not withstanding the dire and widespread poverty everywhere – with sheep on the downs, herds of cattle in the meadows and corn in the fields. They also left their Roman Eagles behind.

Although the Ancient Britons had been left defenceless and denuded in their freedom, they soon got their act together as warriors again as younger people were born and came to maturity, and they fought their subsequent invaders long and hard before being put to flight. As has already been mentioned, the Saxons set about building on the earlier sites of the Romans and Ancient Britons, changing their names, which is how virtually all the places and names in Berkshire became Saxon.

It is against this background that a Berkshire community has become known as Maidenhead today. It was one of several settlements in King Alfred's own county, all riverside settlements in the Thames Valley – including nearby Windsor and Reading – and it was settled by people residing in a place called South Ellington, Elentone people who had previously distanced themselves from the River Thames by three-quarters of a mile in order to escape the flooding but eventually to build their wooden bridge across the river, calling their new community South Ellington, so-called because it was south of Elentone (to this day Maidenhead is prey to dreadful flooding, as we shall see before we are through with this history).

When getting into the tangled roots of any local history in the UK and trying to discover where ancient towns and villages got their names from – as well as where villages came from before they became towns, and which hamlets turned themselves into villages and then into towns and how or why – there is much confusion and contradiction along the way. This is not only because languages and names change in the passage of time, but also because places and documented records vanish or cannot be traced or corroborated, archaeological remains may or may not exist, long-standing families die out or move on and in some cases mayors have mysteriously ceased to exist, leaving towns to operate apparently without mayors, perhaps for decades.

In Maidenhead, it seems that the record has always shown that while the town had local governments for centuries it did not have centuries of mayors, the reason for which seems to have been lost to history. When I began researching this local history of Maidenhead in October 2006, the town council did not know the name of its first mayor or warden (in Elizabethan England mayors were called wardens), but the missing name was discovered as a result of this book, with a little help from the local newspaper, the *Maidenhead Advertiser*.

Nor did it or does it know of the subsequent mayors who immediately followed the first mayor. It knows other things about the early beginnings of Maidenhead, but not how the town arrived at its name, because the distant origins of that name are confused by different versions of the Celtic, Roman, Anglo-Saxon, Norman and English languages, all of which have been spoken in and around Maidenhead and throughout the Thames Valley once upon a time.

It is because of the confused and contradictory nature of history that a lot of people find it frustrating and say that they do not like the subject as they cannot trust it, to which I reply that it is precisely because we cannot trust it – and because, like it or not, we are all lumbered with it – that we must make a careful study of it. If we get most of it right, we are doing well. Confused and contradictory history – unreliable history – is better than no history at all and let's not fret about getting some of the facts wrong from time to time.

When I asked the local council the name of the first mayor of Maidenhead, I was told that, according to its records, the first mayor, in 1685, was a gentleman by the name of Vincent Pawlyn, who was chosen by charter but replaced later that year by Stephen Fisher, who was elected in September 1685, according to council records.

But there must have been mayors before that time, even though they are not included in the town's records, because the town was incorporated in 1582, so there must surely have been a goodly number of mayors in the intervening period until 1685, mustn't there?

Well, maybe there were, maybe there were not, because it is the case that early-English towns had been known to go without mayors during different periods of their history for one reason or another, either because the town's funds ran out or maybe on account of civil war, or internal politicking. Mayors were sometimes appointed by royal charter and other times because they were elected by council members. A mayor appointed by charter may have been swiftly replaced by an elected mayor, or an elected mayor replaced by one appointed by charter! From the distance of centuries it can be hard to get at the truth of such complicated and mysterious matters, either because records are incomplete or because they do not exist at all, and there are always things that local sources do not know, including councils such as the Royal Borough of Windsor and Maidenhead, which deal with local-studies questions very well but cannot – like authors – be expected to know everything.

So I went back to the council and suggested that Vincent Pawlyn could not have been the town's first mayor (the first *known* mayor, maybe, but not the town's very first mayor), and I was delighted to hear from Chris Atkins, the Librarian of Local Information and Studies at the Royal Borough of Windsor and Maidenhead, who emailed me as follows: 'After much searching I have managed to find a reference in the text of the [1582] charter reproduced by the *Maidenhead Advertiser* for its readers in several editions during January and February 1890. The text runs as follows: "We do assign, nominate, constitute and make our Robert Davus, Charles Pagett, John Hartwell, Silvester Peckes, Geoffrey White, Robert Noke, Edward Lockeyre, William Orams, Robert Rodes, Thomas Lambden and Robert Wynche to be and become the first and present burgesses of the town…and we…do assign, nominate, constitute and make our beloved, the aforesaid Robert Davus, one of the burgesses of the town aforesaid, to be and become the first and present warden of the town aforesaid."'

So, thanks to this book, the Royal Borough of Windsor and Maidenhead now has the name of the first mayor or warden of Maidenhead from the time that the town was originally incorporated by Queen Elizabeth I. And Chris Atkins says 'We had no ready reference to Davus's name, just to the charter, and his post. So thank you!'

So Robert Davus was Maidenhead's first mayor – he who was previously missing from the records – but there is so much more to know about him than we do. How interesting it would be to know more about this man called Davus, whose surname is Latin and who may have been of Roman origin, therefore.

All we can say is that the first mayor of Maidenhead had a Latin/Roman surname, rather than a Celtic/Welsh, Anglo-Saxon, Danish or Norman surname, any number of which were fairly common in Maidenhead and other parts of the Thames Valley in those days and still are today.

There is a famous fictional slave called Davus in a classical Italian satire by the Roman poet and satirist Horace, who arranges for Davus to satirise his slave master by telling him some home truths about his social climbing, adultery and gluttony, all of which the slave argues makes the master a slave also. As we have seen, the Ancient Britons were enslaved by the Romans in their time and there must have been inter-breeding between the two sides also, so it is hardly surprising if there are still some Roman names in the Thames Valley as well as some traces of Roman blood, along with all the other Celtic/Welsh, Norman, Danish and Anglo-Saxon blood that has been spilt and inter-mingled there throughout its history. It seems inconceivable that the 'illegitimate' sons of Roman soldiers would not have taken the Roman surnames of their fathers.

Mayor Vincent Pawlyn's appointment as Mayor of Maidenhead recorded by the town council in 1685 comes a century after the appointment of Robert Davus, the first mayor or warden in Elizabethan times, so what did the town do for mayors in the meantime?

Now that we have Davus's name, perhaps there are still more names to be found – between 1582 and 1685 before we get to Pawlyn – and no doubt the council would be pleased to know of them.

There is so much skating on thin ice and so much uncertainty in the telling of local history!

But what we can say with certainty of the early history of Maidenhead – before it was declared a town by Queen Elizabeth I in the 16th century – is that enough archaeological remains have been found to show that Celts, Romans and Saxons lived there in their time, and that there was some kind of fort at Maidenhead Thicket judging from an embankment that was discovered there.

There were also the remains of a Roman Villa in Castle Hill, which came to light in 1886 in the grounds of a property belonging to a local resident called Silver (who may have been Jewish), in which Roman coins, pieces of pottery and animal bones (deer, pigs and sheep) were unearthed, as well as an outline of different rooms of the villa – suggesting a kitchen, bathroom, central heating and so on – complete with a lead pipe from a bath. There are also signs of a Roman road having crossed Maidenhead High Street from north to south, through Kidwell's Park and on to Cookham a little way north of Maidenhead, and even before the Romans we have the remains of pit dwellings and hut circles left behind by Celts. Another Roman Villa was at Cox green. William Camden tells us in his *Britannia* that there 'have been found the ruins of an old castle, and Roman coins are frequently dug up'.

Because written evidence, such as there is for early English history, is still quite patchy and thin on the ground, there are only a few principal sources to which one can turn and information is usually gleaned from the *Domesday Book*, *The Anglo-Saxon Chronicles*, from public records (such as they are) and from the Venerable Bede's *Ecclesiastical History of the English Church and People* in the eighth century, which drew on Papal records from all over the country. When it comes to ancient place names there is the *Oxford Names Companion*, with 15,000 British place names throughout the UK, from Celtic and Old English to Old Scandinavia, as well as 70,000 surnames and 7,000 first names (all very useful).

Of course, in addition to the published sources there are unpublished sources that include place names, public records, church records and archaeological digs, from which clues and possible explanations may be found.

There is also William Camden's aforementioned and widely published *Britannia*, which came much later in the 16th and 17th centuries, and Ralph Holinshed's 16th-century *Chronicles*. But there is virtually nowhere else to go and, very often, clues offered by the earliest written records and by the deeply mysterious, not to say contradictory, place names cannot stand up without some vital bits of concrete evidence from archaeology, which is why these digs are so important and why the source in Castle Street in Maidenhead has turned out to be so very useful indeed. It has yielded verification of Roman life in Maidenhead before it became a town – as opposed to Roman soldiers passing through – once upon a time in the distant past, while also providing us with interesting results about the way these Romans lived, by reason of the implements and other remains that have survived for centuries afterwards.

And while these sources may not sound like very much to go on, it is interesting how one can go far on so little. On the other hand there is much still that we do not know and may never know when going back to early times (in later history the records and the evidence become much more reliable, much better researched, corroborated, written, preserved and understood, as the study of history becomes a seriously academic subject). But thanks to the wonder and persistence of archaeology we can say with certainty what we suspected previously from place names – that the Romans were indeed in Maidenhead, and we know that they were in other parts of Berkshire as well.

We can also say – thanks to the *Domesday Book* in 1086 – that there was a place that was called Elentone, which gave birth to Maidenhead, and that it occupied acres of meadow and woodland that was farmland, complete with cattle, ploughs and cottages. This place seems to have been in the fiefdom of a Norman knight called de Pinckney, after whom the Maidenhead suburb of Pinkney's Green is named, and we know from William Camden in *Britannia,* published in English in 1610, that South Ellington – spelt Southealington – was called 'afterward Maidenhith and at this day Maidenhead.'

So we can deduce from this that the people who built the first wooden bridge over the Thames from which the town of Maidenhead grew, must have been Pinkney's Green and Elentone people (hamlet people), whose pioneering enterprise turned them into a new village when their bridge got them to the other side of the river, a village that became a town known as South Ellington and finally Maidenhead. But I wonder whose brainchild it was? Who was their leader? A hamlet is a small village without a church, and we know that this was indeed a small community that had to go either to Cookham or Bray for a church.

The *Domesday Book* also tells us about Bray: 'King Edward held it. 18 hides, but they did not pay tax. Land for...In lordship 3 ploughs; 56 villagers and 7 smallholders with 25 ploughs. 4 slaves; a church; 3 men-at-arms; meadow, 50 acres; woodland at 60 pigs. Reinbald holds 1 hide which belongs to the church; he has 1 plough there. Value of the whole before 1066 £25, later £18; now £17.'

Imagine Bray today with the monarch owning four slaves there! Fellow English slaves at that! One wonders what was the use of a single hide to Reinbald, a hide that belonged to the church? Did he rent it from the church? Was it on loan? What use was it to him? To keep himself warm maybe? If any readers or local historians know the answer to these questions, how interesting it will be! As we see, this is very sketchy material from which to write and draw conclusions from history, but, even so, it provides some invaluable insights and we should be a lot poorer without such material. We are also told that there were '20 hides' at Cookham, also held by King Edward, 'but it never paid tax', and that there were also '4 slaves' among '32 villagers', where there were '2 mills' and '2 fisheries', etc.

South Ellington – a suburb in the north of Maidenhead today – became Maidenhead after 1296, but today's spelling did not emerge until 1724. The Maidenhead Heritage Centre tells us that some 33 variations of the place name have been found, and we shall look at the most interesting ones in chapter five.

The *Domesday Book* tells us that 'Giles [de Pinkney] holds Elenton. Sieward held it before 1066', and we know from excavations that there were Norman remains there – just one mile northwards from today's town centre, near to North Town Cricket Club. We also know that the Norman Knight de Pinkney had tenanted farmers and peasants living on his land – 12 heads of household with a tiny population of not more than 40–50 overall (while he may have lived as far away as Northamptonshire, according to the Heritage Centre, it would seem that these Pinkney's Green and Elentone people were the original founders of Maidenhead).

A word about *The Anglo-Saxon Chronicles*, the *Domesday Book* and *Britannia*. The former were written by unknown clerics, and they began during the reign of King Alfred the Great in the ninth century, before ending in the 12th century with the coronation of Henry II. Nobody knows why they ended or began, except to say that they began at a time when King Alfred was very much in favour of education and was encouraging it for the first time in English history. Nobody knows who the authors of the *Chronicles* were, but if it were not for these *Chronicles* we should know far less about English history. While they do not read like modern journalism, they were journalism pure and simple, and the first draft of history. While they are nothing more than a collection of dry-as-dust bones with insufficient flesh on them, these sparsely written, terse and tight-lipped *Chronicles* nevertheless provide us with the only record and insight that we have into what was going on in those days, a record that was written while it was all going on, providing us with obtuse scraps of unexplained history that do not piece together very well, if at all (perhaps the authors were not very fluent or well educated). They provide not more than a narrow view through which one strains to see the wider picture (such are the frustrations of historical search), and about which it is all too easy to reach the wrong conclusions.

But, for all that, we can see that the Anglo-Saxons were cultivated and sophisticated enough – by the standards of their time – to have a literature of their own in which they recorded their history meticulously, however tersely expressed without explanation, and that they were disciplined enough to live their lives justly by clearly defined rules and a certain amount of mutual trust.

We can also see that they were warriors extraordinaire, who defended their island heroically – one can hear Winston Churchill's words in his unmistakable voice from World War Two echoing in our ears: 'we shall defend our island' – and they defended it with great determination against the formidable Viking invaders, for which the Anglo-Saxons in the south of England had some kind of national defence system in place, as they fought fearlessly and with a purpose wherever necessary until they had driven the Danes into submission once and for all.

When the Anglo-Saxons lost the Battle of Hastings to the Normans in 1066 – after their amazing warriors had marched all the way from battling in the north of England to the south for another battle there, to confront the Norman invaders as they came off their ships from Northern France – it seems no exaggeration to say that it was a fluky victory for the Normans, who were being successfully deterred until King Harold got that fateful arrow in his eye and his men made the fatal mistake of disobeying his orders, in a moment of madness, and so committed a disastrous defensive error of breaking ranks that cost them and their kingdom greatly. So the Normans won the battle and they were in England to stay. Thinking they had the Normans on the run, the Anglo-Saxons found that they had left a fatal hole in their own defence for others to pour through, and so they were undone.

With the early English and Ancient Britons having fought like tigers against so many invaders from the very beginning of their history – against Romans, Danish Vikings and Normans – it is hardly surprising that they became a martial race early on, just as it is hardly surprising that, having been well and truly colonised by these invaders, they became colonisers themselves in the fullness of time. They learnt both crafts before they became of age and they learnt them well.

There are six parts to *The Anglo-Saxon Chronicles* from the time of the Roman occupation to the Anglo-Saxon invasions, and the coming of Christianity to the early Viking period and the Norsemen, right through to William the Conqueror and the Norman occupation and beyond, before they disappear from the pages of English history for reasons that remain a mystery.

As for the *Domesday Book* – in which an area that we call Maidenhead today can be glimpsed in its records – it was a survey of England ordered by King William I so that he could list all his possessions and assess the value of his estates for the purposes of taxation.

Every property, acre of arable land, ox, cow, pig, chicken, plough, axe and so on was meticulously recorded – the picture of the country and its people was otherwise incomplete in the absence of so much else. However, at least it provides us with something to go on today, without which we would be seriously lost when trying to piece together a picture of the past. With nine out of 10 people living and working in rural communities in those days – and the farming people coming from the Danes and the Saxons rather than the Normans – a picture of sorts begins to emerge.

While some parts of the country – including London and Winchester – were omitted from the survey in this book, for reasons that are not clear, most other places were not, and they had to pay up when the king's commissioners came calling, county by county and manor by manor. The names of landowners and residents were all listed, as were the taxes, rents and services that they owed, and the book was in two massive volumes, currently to be found in the Public Records Office in London. It was a work of royal housekeeping – a fiscal record – from which one can get an idea of who lived where and when in those distant times. It is thanks to this book that we know about the Pinkney's Green and South Ellington tenants in Maidenhead. It would seem that the town that was declared Maidenhead in Elizabethan England, previously began in Pinkney's Green and South Ellington, growing in the fullness of time into a full-blown town with a bridge over the river. The Pinkney's Green/Elentone people eventually came down to the river and founded a prosperous village-cum-town there (having decided not to worry about flooding after all). So here's to them. They did well.

Maidenhead's startling progressions to township would seem to have been, in a nutshell:

(1) Pinkney's Green, Elentone and South Ellington.

(2) A 13th-century wooden bridge over the River Thames.

(3) Maidenhead, a small Elizabethan town in the 16th century.

(4) By The Good Grace of Queen Elizabeth I in the Days of Sir Francis Drake and the Spanish Armada.

Prior to that, Maidenhead's previous surrounding history and regional influences would seem to have been:

(1) A Roman villa in Cox Green from the first to the fourth century.

(2) A Saxon warrior king at Taplow in the seventh century.

(3) A Saxon parliament at Witan at Cookham in the 10th century.

(4) An 11th-century entry in the *Domesday Book* for Bray, Cookham, Pinkney's Green and Elentone.

(5) All-important membership of King Alfred the Great's regional kingdom of Wessex that prevented the Danish Vikings from taking over the country, the county and the town of Maidenhead.

(6) A Norman castle and court at nearby Windsor that was destined to become Windsor Castle.

Maidenhead's startling progression to racial composition seems to have been, in a nutshell:

(1) Ancient Britons.

(2) Romans (there would have been rape and inter-breeding).

(3) Germanic Anglo-Saxons with some Jutland Jutes.

(4) Danish Vikings (there was rape as well as co-habiting).

(5) Normans with some Bretons and Parisians (again there was rape as well as marriage).

(6) English Nationhood by the Good Grace of King Alfred the Great, Henry VIII, his daughter Elizabeth I and the first English Parliament in 1689, which curtailed the royal prerogative and guaranteed freedom of speech and free elections for MPs.

While the above layman's racial analysis applies to most English towns, cities and villages, in some parts of the country there was a greater Celtic, Danish and Jute input – Jutes especially on the Isle of Wight, for some reason – and a smaller Roman and Norman input, and this was before the French Huguenots, Irish and Scots began to settle in the UK.

As we see, England has been a multi-racial society with multi-cultural blood in its veins from way back, and a multi-cultural society that has worked very well.

As far as the so-called Celts are concerned, we now know from recent historical research in Europe that most of the people in Britain and Ireland claiming to be Celts are probably not Celts at all. The latest historical findings are that most of the Celts – who originally came from the German-Hungarian border – finally settled and died out in France and so could not have settled in Wales or Ireland, as has been claimed for centuries, and that the Irish probably took the Celtic culture for their own for reasons of racial, cultural and political identity, even though they were no such thing! According to the latest history out of European university departments – with which there is academic agreement in Dublin and Cardiff – the few Celts that strayed into England probably settled in London and parts of Yorkshire, but never went anywhere near Wales, Ireland or Cornwall!

This only serves to remind us that history is fraught with error and that it invites and is full of all sorts of mistakes. People – including some historians – are inclined to read into it what they prefer to read into it. On the other hand, it is full of accuracy also, which is what makes it such a fascinating and absorbing subject.

But back to our sources for the researching of early English history. As for William Camden's *Britannia*, there is a much later publication in Latin, published in 1587, but it is such an exhaustive work that translated versions of it are a must for any serious researcher of earlier English history. While Camden was writing about the Middle Ages, he was, like the rest of us, delving back into the past in order to write about the present in which he found himself, and he researched and studied many public records and local histories and published many detailed maps (showing the locations of English tribes – all of which had a history of their own reaching back into the past). Camden was a scholar who was born in London in 1551, and he went to St Paul's school in the capital city before going to the University of Oxford between the ages of 15 and 20, but coming down without a degree. He went on to become the headmaster of London's famous Westminster School, and when he completed his *Britannia* it was so wildly successful that it was published six times. In this book he predicted that the Great Plague of London would happen when Saturn was positioned in Capricornus and, remarkably, that is exactly what happened! He also endowed the first chair for the study of history at Oxford University.

Predictably, copies of William Camden's book are antiquarian collectors' items today and his volumes have become such a precious commodity that the London Library's editions are not for loan, but one can go to the library and read them there – four heavy volumes re-published in English in 1806 – after you have signed your life away for them, on account of their being part of the library's rare book collection. Together with the other editions – in Latin – they cannot leave the premises.

When I went to the London Library in the capital city's St James's Square to look up references to Maidenhead and Berkshire, four huge and heavy volumes were carried from a safe in which they were securely locked away for me to sign for and then study in the reading room. Published in translation (from Latin to English) by John Stockdale in London in 1806, they carry the original dedication by Richard Gough to King George, as follows: 'To the patron of the arts and sciences, the father of his people, George III, who has condescended to encourage researches into antiquity; this work, the earliest general account of his kingdoms, is humbly dedicated by his most dutiful subject Richard Gough.'

This is the same George III who came with his family to enjoy a day out at the Maidenhead horse racing course.

Britannia is a very important historical source. It tells us that the 'place' of Maidenhead is of a 'very ancient date', where 'two centuries before' the time that Camden wrote his *Britannia* 'the passage over the river was higher up at Babham's End, but after a wooden bridge was built here it began to have several inns and to outvie its neighbour and mother-town Bray, which is much older.'

As for Holinshed's *Chronicles* in 1577, they are a record of facts and fancies about the Middle Ages without any critical assessment, conclusions or analysis, or indeed much evidence, so they do, of course, leave much to be desired.

The failure of a source to answer many or all of the questions is, in itself, of profound historical significance and interest not only to students and teachers of history, but also to readers of popular histories who can usefully be reminded of where the materials of history come from and how reliable they may or may not be.

These are matters of interest to all who are curious about the processes and researching of history, in addition to the history itself, and for this reason I have given my sources and the considerations to which they give rise in this chapter, sources which have come up with some of the answers to questions about Maidenhead's origins in the following pages of this book.

CHAPTER FOUR

South Ellington Villagers

The neighbourhood of Pinkney's Green today is a suburb of Maidenhead and, as we have seen, it originally began as a tiny settlement of not more than 40–50 inhabitants owing their allegiance to a knight. This much can be gleaned from the *Domesday Book*. In the new millennium there is kite flying at Pinkney's Green, which is located between Maidenhead town centre and the A404 at Maidenhead Thicket (once upon a time a hideaway for notorious highwaymen).

A settlement of 40–50 people doesn't sound like much, but we tend to forget that it was not until the 12th and 13th centuries that the English countryside and its structure of villages and towns began to be settled once and for all in English history. Up until that time, country people were generally scattered in very small and obscure communities that were shifting from place to place and living in hamlets, which did not amount to very much. Small communities tended to huddle together rather than reach out to one another and get together. There was very little economic or social growth in the English countryside.

There was nothing settled or permanent about the early English landscape or community life. People kept to themselves and their own settlements, homesteads and farmsteads, and the fields in which they farmed their cattle were small, not the big open fields with which we are familiar today. Prior to the 12th and 13th centuries there had been a dozen centuries of scenic and social change (listless change, not dynamic growth) of a kind that is not readily imaginable to us in the new millennium, which is why, when explaining the history of a country town such as Maidenhead, that started life as a village built by hamlet people, it is as well to stop and think what was going on in the English countryside in those distant and incomprehensible days. And what was going on was a very hard and unsettled life for most country people, many of whom moved from place to place against the background of a shifting and temporary landscape in which hamlets came and went, not infrequently disappearing without trace.

It is hard for us to imagine this today because we are used to a permanent and settled landscape. We are used to our villages and village greens remaining on the map and not disappearing overnight or, with a few notable exceptions, turning themselves into towns overnight. We are used to villages remaining villages and attracting outsiders to go and live there, and hamlets remaining hamlets. But that was not the case when the 50 or so inhabitants of Pinkney's Green and also of Elentone got themselves recorded for history in the *Domesday Book*. It seems no exaggeration to say that these impoverished inhabitants would have been working very hard in order to be very grateful for some crumbs from Sir Henry de Pinkney's table.

Today we are not generally accustomed to country landscapes and people being shuffled like a pack of cards, as new villages and towns replace hamlets that are no more. When we go into the Thames Valley we usually see what we expect to see and find what we expect to find, but the early inhabitants of Pinkney's Green/Elentone had no idea how long their community would last or how the surrounding countryside might look in the foreseeable future, or that they would turn themselves into William Camden's 'small town in the last age called Southealington, now Maidenhead'.

In bygone days – those of King Alfred the Great and William the Conqueror – the English countryside consisted of impermanent hamlets and farmsteads, many of which were here today and gone tomorrow as people abandoned them in favour of larger villages elsewhere, or other hamlets elsewhere, where they hoped that the grass would be greener, just as the descendants of the Pinkney's Green/Elentone people hoped that the grass would be greener on the other side of the river – the southern, Bray side, where traffic out of London in a westerly direction suggested that they might do a lot better for themselves if they could provide for it. It had to be better than remaining at the mercy of the de Pinkney estate, paying their dues to them! Let others serve them if they wished, but these adventurous people obviously had bigger ideas, if indeed their descendants were the ones who built Maidenhead's first wooden bridge, eventually turning themselves into hamlet and then village people.

In the early history of Maidenhead we have a very clear and interesting example of how populations were shifting in early English history – of how social and scenic change was in the air. The coaching inns and stables that resulted from a wooden bridge over the river at Maidenhead were a dramatically different landscape from the one that had been left behind by these Pinkney's Green and South Ellington bridge builders from the back of beyond. They moved down to a river that they had previously avoided for fear of flooding, and then reached out to the far side of that river where they perceived – correctly as things turned out – that they could indeed have a better life. This is my version of history, not the recorded version, and I make the observation on the logic of probability, knowing what we know of the factual record as well as what we know of people and of what appears to have happened to these people, and the town that they created subsequently.

In this way, these people turned themselves into a new and thriving little village from a hamlet and eventually into a country town no less, that would become a permanent rather than an impermanent feature of their lives in which everything had previously been so temporary, a town where they could become settled at last and where they could also proceed to settle the landscape around them.

There is nothing new about any of this in the developing countries of the world today, where populations are shifting all the time, as are the landscapes, but we tend to forget that it used to go on in England as well. These early Maidenhead people were not unlike the American cowboys who rolled their wagons westward to make a new life for themselves, except to say that the Maidenhead people were centuries ahead of the first European Americans and their 'wild west' was on the other side of a river.

One can well imagine that as a result of successive invasions by Danish Vikings the English countryside was very run down and under a dark cloud for quite a while – positively languishing and in the doldrums – having wasted away for too long with the Roman roads not being maintained, the Roman villas run down and abandoned, the Anglo-Saxon homesteads, hamlets and villages becoming miserably neglected (completely lacking in vitality), as were the money economy and local cottage industries, likewise.

The cumulative effect of these Danish invasions must have been intolerable, so one can well understand that the English needed to get shot of these pesky Danes fast. The Ancient Britons had been invaded by Romans, Picts, Anglo-Saxons and Danes, with the Saxons emerging as top dogs in the wake of the Romans before the Normans arrived on the scene. So early English history did not exactly get off to a brisk social and economic start, which is why there were an awful lot of shifting populations in the country back then, with people living in impermanent hamlets searching for some solid permanence elsewhere, if only on the other side of a river.

We are reminded of this by Richard Muir in his book *The Villages of England*, which provides us with a picture of hamlet people drifting into the new villages that were taking over from England's 'old countryside' of 'small fields and scattered farmsteads'. The English countryside was up for grabs and in the making still, and not least in and around that part of the Thames Valley that we call Maidenhead today. The countryside had not taken shape or firmly established itself, and Muir tells us that King Alfred and the Danish settlements in England were creating 'great social and scenic changes' that continued right throughout the Norman and Plantagenet periods of English history (as we are seeing in these pages, Maidenhead and its surrounding hamlets and villages were, of course, no exception).

These Pinkney's Green/Elentone hamlet dwellers – whoever they were – were certainly pioneers. They had a vision of a wooden bridge across the river and a village that could be established there. Whether they had a vision of a town as well it is impossible to say. Probably not. The chances are that these backwoodsmen and their families had never visited or seen any towns in their lives. The village that the Pinkney's Green, Elentone and South Ellington people turned themselves into became known as Maidenhythe and then Maidenhead; the rest, as they say, is history.

Four centuries after the arrival of the ninth-century Vikings, the enterprising villagers of South Ellington had built themselves a wooden 13th-century bridge across the Thames in order to put themselves in a position to prosper from the great western escape route from London to Bath and Bristol via Reading, on a road that is currently the A4.

On the other southern side of the river from South Ellington these villagers provided for regular travellers – horsemen and horse-drawn coaches – with money to spend on inns, stables, blacksmiths, vets and breweries, and feeding and watering for both man and beast. Given that they had chosen a location that was one day's journey from London at that time, these villagers were very well placed to offer overnight accommodation on outward and return journeys, monopolising all the trade that was there for the taking. This, in turn, was good for the farming and agricultural community and a goodly number of other South Ellington small businesses, and not least for brewers of beer. In due course the small town of Maidenhead had no less than four breweries! But let's not forget that in the absence of clean water most families were obliged to drink beer.

How one would love to know so much more about the original builders of Maidenhead's first bridge across the river, and who it was that was behind the project and the driving force for it? What canny entrepreneurs they seem to have been. Such foresight! Since the bridge was wooden, they must have been very good carpenters. Before they completed the building of their bridge in 1250, the westward road out of London had been diverted up to Cookham on the northern side of the river, before finding its way back down again to Maidenhead Thicket on the Reading side, from where it went west to Bath and Bristol via Reading.

Travellers had presumably been going up to Cookham previously because that was the nearest place where they could have a rest and find accommodation for the night. But after the building of Maidenhead's wooden bridge and the coaching inns and stables that came with it, a more direct route was suddenly provided for travellers out of London, travellers who no longer had to take the circuitous route up to Cookham in order to arrive down at Maidenhead Thicket again. Instead, they avoided the northern side of the river completely and went straight through 'Maidenhythe' on the southern side, to the thicket and beyond to Reading. But had these early hamlet people not come from the northern side and built their bridge, then there would have been no place for London travellers to have stayed over on the southern side, on a direct route to the West Country.

So these bridge builders had successfully diverted traffic and trade from

Cookham into their own neck of the woods because it made more sense for the travellers coming out of and going up to London, and, as we can see from the comparative commercial importance of Maidenhead and Cookham today, Maidenhead has never looked back since. Cookham has lagged behind, but on the other hand it has not been spoilt by progress and modernisation anywhere near as much as Maidenhead, and it is a much prettier, more fashionable and residential place. The history of Maidenhead has been chiefly about commerce and the uglier aspects of the architecture and environment of commerce, but not so in Cookham (or Bray for that matter – also left behind by Maidenhead).

This was clever and opportunistic thinking from the founders of modern Maidenhead. Not only had they brough   erto unimagined prosperity to their own village community, which   y was beginning to thrive and take off for a change, but they had also provided an essential link in a long chain of communications between London and the West Country. They were the forerunners to all commerce and enterprise in Maidenhead today. And not for nothing were numerous royal grants made by different monarchs to keep their wooden bridge in good shape and working order in generations to come, because the strategic importance of it to keeping the infrastructure of the kingdom together was obvious to these monarchs (many of whom had horse soldiers and foot soldiers in need of passing over it).

The bridge did break down, as wooden bridges did in those days, but it was quickly patched up again. We have heard that Kings James I, for example, granted oak trees annually from his royal estates – probably from Cookham and Bray – to ensure that there was enough wood for regular repair work to be carried out, and in order to pay for the upkeep of the bridge a hermit was installed to collect moneys from those who used it.

In the Middle Ages this was common practice and there were hermits on or adjacent to bridges in most riverside communities, who lived in free accommodation in a specially-built little hermitage, with or without a chapel, fitted to the bridge across the river. These hermits took a solemn vow to commit themselves to a life of religious devotion and renunciation, and, in return for living in the free accommodation provided, they collected tolls from travellers – moneys that were then handed over to diocese bishops after each hermit had taken just enough for his own sustenance. Hermits were priests or laymen, and we know that Richard Ludlow was appointed to a hermitage at Maidenhead Bridge on 29 October 1423 by John Warden, from the Collegiate Church of Shottesbrook, who had been sent by the Bishop of Salisbury to swear Ludlow in, 'in the name of God'. This swearing in was quite a ceremonial affair, with local dignitaries and no doubt members of the general public attending the event. All this was more than a century before Maidenhead became a town.

The social and economic history of river bridges in the UK and their contribution to the outcome of regional and national events is a massively overlooked subject by social and other historians. One looks in vain for any reference to the importance of river bridges in the works of our greatest social historians – G.M. Trevelyan (*English Social History: A Survey of Six Centuries*), Asa Briggs (*A Social History of England*) and Christopher Hibbert (*The English: A Social History, 1066–1945*) – and, of the three, only Hibbert deals with rivers, but not in relation to the significance of their bridges. Yet the social fabric and prosperity of towns like Maidenhead is all to do with that all-important bridge across the river, without which there would have been no town, but there is no mention either of bridges or of Maidenhead in these standard works (as we see, different things appeal to the imaginations of different historians).

While Hibbert reminds us that Oxfordshire wool was sent by river to London from Henley-on-Thames, and observes that major mediaeval towns were all on rivers and had wharfs that catered for water-borne traffic, with cargo boats and passenger boats constantly coming and going, he neglects to analyse the bridges from the point of view of their economic or sociological significance, let alone their historical significance within the communities where they were to be found, and without which there would, in many cases, have been no communities. Probably he takes it for granted that we realise this without any emphasis from him. He neglects to tell us how these bridges came about and the difference they made both regionally and nationally, not least in such a place as the Thames Valley, where there are more bridges and riverside communities than most.

The people of the Thames Valley are a tribe of river people and bridge builders if ever there was.

As we can see from this little history of Maidenhead, its small wooden bridge made a huge difference both locally, regionally and nationally. It gave birth to a town, it connected a locality to a region more efficiently than hitherto and it contributed to an important national infrastructure, not simply an infrastructure of river traffic but of road traffic also, between London and the West Country, where rail traffic would follow in due course. In short, it put a town on the map, making a very big difference to the routes to be found on the map itself, and it attracted the attention and financial support of royalty.

One cannot stress too much the importance of this 13th-century wooden bridge.

Of course, a stone and a railway bridge came to Maidenhead later – as we shall see before we are through – but without his wooden bridge there would have been no village of 'Maidenhythe', or town of Maidenhead. Nor would there have been any need for such a community there, no emergence of a thriving and thrusting community, and no need for a symbolic maiden to have figured in the name of Maidenhead.

CHAPTER FIVE

What's in a Name?

There are all sorts of intriguing theories about where the name Maidenhead came from, not that anybody knows for sure. Reference has already been made in chapter one to the inadequate explanation given in the *Oxford Names Companion*, which claimed that Maidenhead meant, in Old English (1202), 'A Landing Place for Maidens.'

This begs the question, which maidens? But, don't ask, because nobody knows who they were or where they came from or why they wanted to land, or whether in fact they did land. It also raises serious doubts about whether this place name has anything to do with maidens whatsoever, as there are other theories on offer.

The esteemed William Camden, who was much closer to these events than we, wrote in his *Britannia* that the name of Maidenhead came from a 'veneration' paid to 'I know not what British virgin, one of the 11,000 who returning home with Ursula from Rome were martyred at Cologne in Germany by Attila the Scourge of God.'

There is a 14th-century maidens-head seal, a printed image that appears every week on the *Maidenhead Advertiser*, which was the town's seal from the 16th century until 1910, when it was discontinued for some reason. A golden seal, known as The Godayn Seal, it is the possession of the Royal Borough of Windsor and Maidenhead and went on public display at the Maidenhead Heritage Centre in 2006. There is the face of a maiden with flowing hair in the centre of this seal – which is mounted on ivory (the ivory must have come long after the 14th century) – and this angelic face is encircled by a Latin inscription that reads 'The Seal of John Goldayn, Canon of Thiers', a place that is in the South of France.

Now the question is what on earth did a holy canon from the South of France have to do with Maidenhead, and did it take its name from his seal? Nobody knows how his seal finished up in Maidenhead. Of course, it could have come over – he could have come over perhaps – with the Norman French after they invaded in 1066, or a Norman soldier could have been carrying his seal for some reason. The fact that it became the town's official seal for two to three centuries surely suggests – doesn't it? – that most people in local government were satisfied that Maidenhead's maiden was from the South of France, and that they assumed the town must have taken its name from there. But could they have been wrong? Could this have been an extraordinary coincidence? We need to know much more about the Thiers connection and this French canon, but my publisher, alas, does not have the budget to send me to the South of France to find out. However, it would be interesting to hear from French antiquarian scholars and well-informed others on this subject.

The trouble with different theories that arise at different moments in time in relation to place names and other concerns of local history is that, all too often, they arise in isolation and in ignorance of other matters and theories that went before. For example, one theory may be arrived at in ignorance of another, unchallenged by another. Only in the fullness of time can these theories be challenged with the benefit of hindsight, and even then they are frequently challenged with insufficient knowledge or understanding of what went before. So the issue becomes blurred and confused by contradictory theories good and bad!

Even so, we must stay with the theories and use our own judgement as to which has the logic of probability on its side. The history of Maidenhead is rooted in much agonising over its blessed maiden!

One of the theories is that it is a reference to the Virgin Mary, another, as William Camden has suggested, that the town was named after no less than 11,000 virgins who followed St Ursula and were savagely massacred by Huns in Germany (and doubtless raped into the bargain) on their pilgrimage to Rome in the fourth century, and another that the town was named after virginal nuns at the nearby riverside hamlet of Cookham. There is also the theory that, having built themselves a wooden bridge, the villagers of South Ellington needed a riverside landing stage for the mooring, loading and unloading of their boats, so they built themselves a new (maiden) wharf (hythe) as well, calling their community

'Maidenhythe' in consequence, after their new wharf, just as, in London for example, other wharfages had hythe in their place names – such as Rotherhithe and Greenhithe.

Yet another theory is that the community may have called itself Mid or Midden Hythe to signify that its riverside wharf was 'midway' between Windsor and Marlow or Reading, so Midden may have become Maiden as times, pronunciations and spellings changed.

By the same token, the community may have called itself Maidenhythe or Maidenhead because it became a landing stage for maidens. Maybe this was the wishful thinking of the local male population!

There is also a theory that because the old word for fort is Mai Dun, then the name Maiden comes from the fort at the headland of Maidenhead Thicket – and, therefore, has nothing to do with maidens – or that the Celtic Ma-y-Din-Heth (also on record) was a name given by the Ancient Britons who settled there before the Romans.

English legend has it that the Maid Margaret was pure, virginal, virtuous, especially pure of heart and full of humility – no milk maid this! – but according to H. Bayley, author of *Archaic England*, it is 'probable' that Maidenhead – 'originally Madenheith' – took its name from Maidenheath, named after a meadow or heath sacred to maidens.

But this is to ignore the fact that the seal of the diocese of Salisbury, which was responsible for the upkeep of the wooden bridge that breathed the original life into early Maidenhead, has a symbolic maiden of the sun and the moon on its seal, in which case who is to say that Maidenhead did not take its name from this seal and the image of its maiden for a symbol of its own and incorporate her into its own identity (Bayley does not make this connection, presumably because he did not know about the upkeep of the wooden bridge by the Bishop of Salisbury).

Clearly, the permutations on this place name are endless and far from simple!

As for the 11,000 virginal maidens who followed St Ursula – a British princess and her husband who were supposed to have been returning from Rome when they suddenly got themselves massacred by Huns in Germany at Cologne – well, what can one say? Did this story capture the imaginations of the people of Maidenhead, who named their town after these unfortunate maidens who went to their hearts having been reportedly decapitated by the bows and arrows of the Huns? We are told that Ursula and her virgins were all buried in Cologne where there is a church dedicated to her and which can be visited to this day. While there is absolutely no evidence for Maidenhead having named itself after these ill-fated nuns – or for any of the other explanations given for the place name of Maidenhead – we are nevertheless reminded how events in Germany and Italy may have influenced the choice of name of a quiet English country town, and of how a quiet English country town could have been mindful of and moved by what was going on in far-away Europe. We can see how international history can and sometimes does influence local history, and this in turn enables us to see local history in a new light. This massacre must have been quite an outrage at the time – one can imagine the outrage that such a thing would cause today – and the hearts of people in Maidenhead must have gone out to these massacred nuns, whether or not they named their town after them.

The problem for any historian – local or otherwise – in knitting all these fascinating details together, in order to arrive at a complete and accurate picture, is that for every strand that he or she threads that makes, or appears to make, sense, there is all to often some other strands to make un-sense or nonsense of their work!

For whatever reason, the town was named as it was, with the different spellings blurring the issue. One can finish up like a dog chasing its tail trying to get to the bottom of this riddle.

Considering that Elizabeth I was known as the 'virgin queen', it seems entirely fitting, as things turned out, that the town should have been called Maidenhead, but the allusion to the widely-assumed virginal condition of the queen may have been purely co-incidental when the name for the new town of Maidenhead was being chosen.

On the other hand, it may not have been pure co-incidence.

Let's not forget that after Henry VIII broke away from the Church of Rome, destroying all the Catholic imagery, the biblical Virgin Mary was no longer the bees knees with the populace in Britain, and when Henry's daughter Queen Elizabeth came to the throne new images of her 'virginal' (i.e. maidenly) face were introduced and tightly controlled (on pain of death if you didn't watch out), exclusively issued by her court who put the word about that she was a Virgin Queen, no less.

If believed, this could just as easily have made her some kind of goddess among Protestants, not unlike the Virgin Mary among Catholics before her, so it is well within the realms of possibility that, in place of the Virgin Mary, the powers that be gave the English masses a Virgin Queen instead, their very own Virgin Mary – their very own maiden – to be revered and unquestioned at all times!

I find it surprising that this is not one of the theories put forward for the place name of Maidenhead, in view of the queen having granted the town its status, and also in view of the likelihood of the religious masses in her kingdom being entirely amenable to another mother figure after the older biblical one was removed from the scene.

It would have suited the authorities and the royal court very well to have had their Virgin Queen on a par with the Virgin Mary in the eyes of their people, replacing the previous image of holier than though 'Mary Mother of God' that had been formerly promoted by the Christian Church in England.

Not that those concerned would have put this on record or made a big song and dance about it. And the Queen's image was being promoted for the same political reasons that the Virgin Mary's image had been promoted previously, while Elizabeth and her court were now in a position to benefit from the promotion of a remarkably similar holier-than-though image of a virginal mother caring for her child.

Queen Elizabeth I, mother of her kingdom!

This mother-figure image was not an original Christian idea. On the contrary, it had been used by some pagan religions including that of the Egyptian goddess Isis. The popular idea of a pure and virginal mother caring for her child – whether as mother of Christ or as mother of her nation in the case of Queen Elizabeth I who, like all English monarchs, was supposed to be queen by 'divine right' – would certainly have made excellent political sense when the maidenly Virgin Queen came to the throne as an out and out Protestant rather than a Catholic ruler. And it would have made even more sense when she granted township to the former Thames-side village of Maidenhead, the place name of which could have had 'maiden' inserted in its title in honour of the Queen that had given the town its head, as it were, a virginal maiden's head.

While the place name of the town already had reference to a maiden in it before Queen Elizabeth came to power – if, indeed, the reference was to a maiden rather than a midden (halfway) – that is no reason why Queen Elizabeth's wise men might not have advised her to insist on this maiden (rather than a midden) image as a condition of granting the status of township to this riverside village going for growth.

In which case, the reference in Maidenhead might well have referred to Queen Elizabeth when Robert Davus became the first warden/mayor. Let us not also forget that we are talking 'Royal Berkshire' here – with the royal connection at Windsor since the time of the Norman King, William the Conqueror, who built his castle there – so there would have been, as there has always been, a ready and willing identification with royalty in these parts, including Maidenhead, of course.

This is a new and entirely speculative theory that I am putting forward here and, as I say, all these theories are pure speculation, because nobody can know the answer to such questions from such an ill-recorded distance. But it is food for thought for those who are intrigued by such matters.

In favour of the maiden theory, purely in terms of language, are such considerations as maiden meaning fresh and new, as it still does in our language today in some contexts – and this was a fresh and new town that we were talking about – maiden meaning there had been plenty of fictional and factual maidens around to inspire such a name, maidens who may very well have used South Ellington's new wharf as a landing stage, or have captured the public imagination locally without their necessarily going anywhere near the wharf. Against the maiden theory is the argument that this reference to a maiden in the name of the town was always meant to be midden, not maiden, signifying the fact that the wharf was midway between Windsor and Marlow or Reading, and since the community was once called

'Middenhythe', how could the word hythe (for wharf) possibly have become mistranslated into head instead?

But against both of those theories is the Mai Dun fort theory on the headland of Maidenhead Thicket.

The fact that the record shows that the town was first called Middenhythe – to signify that it was a midway wharf – does suggest that it was not intended to be called Maidenhead (who is to say that a name change was not recommended?), but the point is that it got called Maidenhead before it was through and nobody seems to know why. There is no record of how or why it became Maidenhead and it is curious indeed that a town that was previously known as 'Midway Wharf' suddenly got called Maidenhead, accidentally or otherwise. Certainly, Maidenhead is a better place name than Mid or Midway Wharf, so perhaps that it why it was changed?

Too many theories and not enough facts!

The new bridge and the wharf from which everything began for the town that was built by the villagers of Pinkney's Green/Elentone (Ellenton or Aylington) from the north side of the river, is of more interest than where the name of the town came from. As we have seen, the reason they wanted their bridge was to reach out for commercial reasons to the London to Bristol road (Bath Road) on the south side of the river from their northern enclave. There was money to be made from this road, with all its horsemen and horse-drawn coaches and their weary travellers in need of feeding, watering and an overnight stay, who were still a day's travelling distance from London in those days. So a community of innkeepers, pub landlords, brewers, blacksmiths, vets, stable managers and shop owners eventually grew into the new community of Maidenhythe, or Maidenhead as we know it today, before becoming recognised as a town in the 16th century. This is how it put itself on the map. Nobody else did it. It did it for itself.

One can imagine the excitement when Maidenhead came to manhood, as it were, in 1582, which was one year after Sir Francis Drake had circumnavigated the globe and six years before he led the defeat of the Spanish Armada in 1588. It had taken four years for Drake to circumnavigate the globe, which did not seem like a lifetime back then when time stood still for a great many people.

It had taken some three centuries for Maidenhythe to grow slowly from a village into a town in which most people stayed put, just as they did, of course, elsewhere in the country, unless they got press-ganged into the navy or joined the army, the exception being rich people who could afford a horse and carriage, given that they were not deterred by highwaymen.

Since distant places and the ends of the earth were the other side of the moon to most people in Elizabethan England, Drake's awesome and almost certainly incredible circumnavigation of the globe in only four years was probably seen by most ordinary, stay-at-home people as swift indeed.

In addition to its mayor, town corporation, street markets and fairs, Maidenhead got a court with a justice system and some bridge masters. So things were looking up for the town in Elizabethan times. It had bounce in its step.

There had also been a chaplain of St Mary Magdalene's Church and Guild in Maidenhead since 1451, and it was the chaplain of the church who, in addition to being responsible for the chauntry (an endowment or chapel for the chanting of holy mass), is said to have been responsible for the upkeep and good working order of the wooden bridge over the river before Maidenhead became a town. This church remains the borough council church to this day and can be found in St Mary's Close just off the High Street, and its vicar is still the 'Mayor's Chaplain', who takes prayers on the first Sunday after the mayor has taken office each year, attended by the corporation and its mayor, while also holding ceremonial services for Remembrance Day and Battle of Britain Day, but not for Defeat of the Armada day (nor is he held responsible for Maidenhead Bridge).

The history of Maidenhead is absolutely rooted in its river, its bridge, its church, the kings and queens of England and its legendary maiden. Maidenhead originally prospered with a brisk trade in malt for the brewing industry, timber for so many industries, meal from coarsely ground grain for the cereals and animal-feed industries, and innkeeping, catering and stabling for the Great Western coaches that thundered through its high street. But it remained a one-street town until the latter 19th century (it never ceases to amaze one how much lucrative business a single street can generate).

This is a history that was, as we shall see, accelerated later on by the coming of the railways in Victorian Britain.

CHAPTER SIX

A Cock and Bull Story

According to William Camden, the new coaching town of Maidenhead was soon in competition with its neighbour Bray. Camden tells us that Maidenhead had built 'a wooden bridge upon piles' and that it soon began to be 'so frequented as to outvie its neighbouring mother, Bray, a much more ancient place'.

But the mystery is what took Maidenhead High Street so long to get its first coaching inns? There appears to be no record of a coaching inn in Maidenhead High Street until 1459 – the bridge was completed before 1300 – if Bray Court Rolls are anything to go by, showing an inn called the 'Bulle' to be in the ownership of a William Murdall, later to be succeeded by an Alice Buckland in 1489. It is so unusual to see a liberated female entrepreneur in 15th-century Maidenhead – so Alice Buckland is yet another that one would love to know more about – a century and a half ahead of the first female entrepreneurs in the Middle Ages. In her book *The Weaker Vessel: Woman's Lot In 17th Century England*, Antonia Fraser tells us that she wrote her book in answer to the question (put to her by a distinguished 20th-century male), 'Were there any women in 17th century England?'

Well there seems to have been one very enterprising Alice Buckland in 15th-century England, way before the 17th century, and the chances are that in Elizabethan times – with a strong and able Queen on the throne who was more than a match for the men around her – things may have been easier for women than they became later on in the 17th century and beyond. But the historical record for women only seems to begin in the 17th century, which is a pity as it would be good to know more about the role of entrepreneurial 15th-century women and of Maidenhead's Alice Buckland in particular.

It was at the entrance to St Ives Place at number 11 Maidenhead High Street in those days that the Bull Inn stood, and it remained there until the late 19th century when, in 1870, a certain Mr William Wilberforce, the brother of the celebrated Bishop of Oxford (yes, bishops were celebrated in those days), took the Bull for his own and turned it into a chapel with a house for a priest, discontinuing the licence, of course.

Actually, St Ives' Place was named after the Manor of Ive that was, once upon a time, owned by John Ives, who had been legally summoned for fishing in the Thames at Maidenhead back in 1297 (so there was no connection with St Ives in Cornwall). It was Wilberforce who changed the name to St Ives' and it was his brother Samuel Wilberforce who was Bishop of Oxford in 1845 – and of Winchester in 1869 – and was best remembered for having asked T.H. Huxley in an 1860 debate on Darwinism (anathema to the Church of England) whether Huxley was descended from an ape on his grandmother's or grandfather's side!

T.H. Huxley was a biologist and philosopher who had also qualified as a surgeon, and, as a friend of Charles Darwin, he challenged orthodox theology while also coining the term 'agnosticism' (he was furthermore a president of the Royal Society and grandfather of the famous satirical novelist Aldous Huxley of *Brave New World* fame).

We are told by Harold Clunn in his book *The Face of the Home Counties*, published in 1936, that the phrase 'cock and bull story' came about as a result of people observing and frequenting Maidenhead's Bull Hotel – the town's first presumably – a few yards away from a rival which was called The Cock. The drunken and exaggerated gossip that was spoken in and between these two places was referred to as 'cock and bull', on account of its being unreliable and unworthy.

This is either a cock and bull story or it isn't!

But it sounds plausible enough with two such rival inns called Cock and Bull.

Clunn also notes that there was a parish church (St Giles) opposite the premises of both the Cock and the Bull, but I hasten to add that he does not suggest that there was any cock and bull spoken in that church! But it might apply to some, if not several, of the theories put forward for the meaning and origin of the town's place name!

Clunn tells us that St Giles was the companion church of St Mary

Magdalene up the street and that it caught fire in 1742, which was so terrible that two thirds of the east side of the high street was also destroyed (he does not tell us what caused the fire). Only the church tower – dating from the time of Edward I – survived this fire. The preservation of this tower, Clunn observes, gave a false impression when walking down the hill into Maidenhead from the London side of the town of their being two churches in the high street when there was only one, with the solitary tower of St Giles standing 'forlorn by itself' in line with a solitary tree standing in the market square behind where St Giles's Church had stood before it was burned to the ground.

Harold Clunn's book, published in 1936 by the quaint-sounding firm of Simpkin Marshall Limited (no longer in existence) of Stationer's Hall Court in the City of London, is dedicated even more quaintly to 'the recreation and enjoyment of my fellow citizens', and one likes to feel that those who built Maidenhead's original wooden bridge, which breathed life into this town that had not existed previously, were dedicating their town to the recreation and enjoyment of their fellow citizens.

Of course, they were essentially making their bid for freedom from the dreary riverside backwoods (now neat and tidy suburbs) and lining their own pockets in the process, but they were also creating something of recreation and enjoyment for others besides, not least those who booked into the Bull Hotel, or 'Bulle' Inn as it was originally called in the days before standard English and consistent spelling.

With or without its cock and bull, Maidenhead had arrived and there was no looking back. It was an important coaching and market town that was close enough but not too close to London to fulfil a useful function for travellers going east and west between the capital city and Bristol, the latter which was one of the most important cities in England and for a time the second most important after London. With Maidenhead's cobbled high street (the cobbles are long gone) one can well imagine the noisy clatter of horses hooves and coach wheels up and down this thoroughfare all day long en route to Bristol and also to London by return – sometimes as many as 90 coaches a day, as we have observed.

This was hitherto unimagined excitement and prosperity for the people of Maidenhead. All very impressive. There were coaching inns and pubs all over early Maidenhead, including the Greyhound, Bear, Swan, White Horse, Saracen's Head, Lion, Sun, Fighting Cocks, Fox & Horn, Crown, Kings Arms, White Hart, Fleece, Windsor Castle, Quart Pot and Folly, to mention but a few. The coaching inn business and brewery business in Maidenhead were very big business indeed and what helped, initially, to put the town on the map. There was also the Orkney Arms, which became the famous and glamorous Skindle's Hotel at Maidenhead Bridge, frequented by Berkshire toffs, including Eton College rich kids and their parents from the nearby borough of Windsor and Eton, and the occasional member of royalty.

Okay, so Maidenhead had arrived 337 years after the incorporation of the nearby Berkshire town of Reading in 1245, and 512 years after neighbouring Windsor in 1070. But while these towns are considerably older than Maidenhead, the latter had nevertheless arrived as an invigorating new boy on the block in a place where nothing was happening previously, overshadowing both Bray and Cookham into the bargain, putting their noses out of joint, relieving Cookham of quite a lot of trade, and causing Reading and Windsor to sit up and pay attention.

There was no holding Maidenhead back now, as it made its mark, which is doubtless why eyebrows were being raised in both Reading and Windsor (as for Slough, it was still a sleepy little village snoozing away, and it would not become a modern industrial estate and town until much later).

So Maidenhead had invented itself, stolen a march on its rivals in Bray (its mother) and Cookham, and it was all down to its being perfectly and conveniently placed to do so – one day's journey from London – and down furthermore to its enterprising bridge builders spotting their opportunity and going for it.

Of course, Maidenhead would never be as royal, influential or quite as big as Windsor, or as commercially important or as big as Reading, but it was on its way and that's all that mattered. Nor would it be a university town like Reading, or a royal town with a magnificent castle like Windsor – the largest inhabited castle in Europe today – where so much history had been made by the Norman King William who built the castle in the first place and by the subsequent monarchs who stayed there, within whose stone walls a great library had and has to this day the whole history of England encased there. And let's not forget all those rich aristocratic kids at Eton College who supposedly won the Battle of Waterloo on their playing fields (but not a goodly number of other battles alas), the sons of the powerful and famous, the future officer class and government ministers for centuries, none of whom, or whose families, were found to be making history in Maidenhead only a few miles away.

Reading, by far the biggest town in Berkshire, was well placed to be the county's capital town. It had plenty of coaching inns of its own but it wasn't just commercially important in early English history, it was religiously and strategically important as well. While it wasn't as old or as royal as the more fashionable Windsor, Reading was also militarily important. There was a defensive castle in Reading at the top of Castle Hill. The hill is still there on the western side of the town, but minus the castle and any of its remains.

Built on the banks of two rivers at the confluence of the Thames and the Kennet, Reading was well placed as a road, waterway and eventually railway junction, not just between east and west but north and south also. It was a big market town with a magnificent and famous, not to say highly influential, Benedictine Abbey, the ruins of which can be visited today in the town's Forbury Gardens (next door to which I had occasion to work, back in the 1950s, for the local law firm of Blandy & Blandy, when I was studying law). In Forbury Road alongside the Abbey and these gardens there was, back in the 18th century, a girls' school called Reading Ladies Boarding School (now Abbey School), run by a French émigré Mrs Latournelle, which occupied two rooms over the gateway of the Abbey. It is there that Jane Austen and her elder sister, Cassandra, went to school, as did Mary Mitford in the 19th century, after the school had relocated to another part of town.

Since it had been originally incorporated as a town more than 300 years ahead of Maidenhead, Reading was ahead of the game. Supposedly named after the Anglo-Saxon Readda, this place of Readda's people is among the top ten shopping cities in the UK today. King Charles I was captured at Reading and locked up in Caversham House. The celebrated marriage of John O'Gaunt was held in Reading Abbey, which was equal to or greater than Salisbury Cathedral, and the scholastic Henry I, his Queen and his daughter are buried there – but all of this is another story.

While there was no comparison between Maidenhead and Reading – or indeed with Windsor, with all its royal connections – Maidenhead was still becoming an important town in its own right, and only by contrasting and comparing it with other Berkshire towns can one understand the size of its achievement and the rapid progress that it made, coming from nowhere in the doomed Domesday country of Pinkney's Green/Elentone to somewhere in the Elizabethan Age and later on.

However, because Reading and Windsor had been in existence a lot longer and with more things happening in those places, it stands to reason that they had more history to make, but that does not take away from the startling history that Maidenhead was suddenly making from the 13th to the 16th century and beyond. The history of all these Berkshire towns had been interconnected and to some extent inter-reliant, at least militarily, and Maidenhead was becoming an important new part of the jigsaw.

Unlike Windsor, which had its castle and so much of its history handed to it on a plate, Maidenhead had to really work at inventing itself and making its mark. And, unlike Reading, Maidenhead did not have an Abbey, a seat of learning (Reading University, albeit chiefly agricultural learning in the early days) and bigger businesses on its side. Maidenhead came in from the outside, as it were, and was invented by its own hand and out of its own imagination, not out of the imagination of an invading king at Windsor with the clout of his royal household and armies behind him, not to mention a goodly number of Normans already in England before the conquest, who were very influential and strong, and ready to give William the Conqueror their full and instant backing. The fact that a relatively few well-organised Normans could build castles all over England and hold the country in their grip shows how weak and poorly organised Saxon England was at that time and how better off the Norman garrison and other towns were compared with the others, such as Maidenhead. With hunting in mind, William the Conqueror liked Windsor for its forest and parkland, and when he put Windsor Castle in place there – as a stockaded earthwork – he greatly increased the historical importance of Windsor, where the castle would see many additions by subsequent monarchs – several of whom were buried in the castle chapels. When, in the 16th and 17th centuries, the castle began to be converted from a fortress to a palace reaching its zenith under Charles II, and later on in the 19th century, there was no looking back for Windsor, which really had been put on the map by English royalty.

Maidenhead, by comparison, had to struggle to put itself on the map, as had Reading, albeit with the influential but short-lived assistance, once upon a time, of the aforementioned Reading Abbey during a brief period that certainly gave Reading a head-start on other Berkshire towns. Reading Abbey, founded by King Henry I, was dedicated to the Virgin Mary and St John the Evangelist, and it had kept strictly to the rule of St Benedict. Monks from Cluny in France came flooding into the abbey, just as favours, influence and some wealth to kick-start the town also came in as a result of there being an abbey in Reading, the church of which was consecrated by no less a person than Thomas Becket, whose ugly fate with Henry II was not unlike the fate of the abbey itself when it fell from grace for refusing to acknowledge the supremacy of monarchs in spiritual and religious matters (matters other than secular). But in its hey day, kings and their nobles went to Reading Abbey, as did the Patriarch of Jerusalem who travelled all the way to this Berkshire town in 1185 to plead in vain with King Henry II to rescue the Holy Land from the Muslims. The high-society wedding of John O'Gaunt – to the daughter (Blanche) of Henry Plantagenet – was held in the Abbey. There is nothing in the history of Maidenhead to compare with this, just as there is little to compare with Windsor and its royal castle, yet Maidenhead continued to thrive and prosper for all that, with its coaching inns and all the business that they generated.

CHAPTER SEVEN

Replacing a Wooden Bridge with a Stone One

Because Maidenhead's wooden bridge fell into a state of continual disrepair, needing more and more oaks from the royal estates at Cookham and Bray in order to repair it – no less than 20 oak trees at the last count in 1735 – it was replaced by a stone bridge in 1777, reminding the people of Maidenhead of the crucial importance of their bridge across the river. As the *Companion into Berkshire* has since observed, the town of Maidenhead had already become a 'fascinating study of the effects of routes on the rise of a township'.

However, the wooden bridge could not last forever, so along came the English architect Robert Taylor, who had designed Lincoln's Inn in London, where he was the architect to the Bank of England until his death in 1788, while also sculpting the proud monument in Westminster Abbey to England's governor warrior in India, Lord Cornwallis – he who defeated the French at Pondicherry and elsewhere in British India. Taylor was an Essex man who also made some architectural alterations to number 10 Downing Street. A former sculptor and stonemason, he christened his son Michael Angelo Taylor, who was buried, like his father before him, in St Martin's-in-the-Field off London's Trafalgar Square.

In the university city of Oxford, Robert Taylor founded his Taylorian Institute, and it was he who designed a stone bridge that was opened to the public in Maidenhead in 1777 at a cost of some £19,000, for which a mortgage was raised against future tolls and land rents in order to recover the cost. But when these costs had been more than recovered, over a century later, these tolls and rents were suddenly regarded as iniquitous in 1903 when another Mr Taylor – Joseph Taylor from nearby Eton – publicly declared that the tolls were an outrage and that he would drive his car across the bridge in defiance of them.

But, alas, it was not to be because the bridge master locked the toll gates and wouldn't let him through, so he paid up, but, as soon as he got onto the bridge in his motor car with two passengers accompanying him, we are told that he made a speech to a crowd of 500 people who had turned out to cheer him on, declaring that 'The King's Bench will avenge the King's Highway', and so it did because Maidenhead Bridge was made free of tolls in 1903 when cheering crowds pulled the old toll gate down and chucked it into the river at the stroke of midnight on 31 October – taking care to remove the toll house clock to the public library. Since the people of Maidenhead and those passing through the town had paid tolls for too long, they figured, quite rightly, that they had more than repaid the original debt and should not be required to pay anymore. So they simply refused to pay and got shot of the tolls with the same determination that had helped to get shot of the Vikings and their *Danegeld* back in the ninth century.

Taylor's bridge has 13 arches, five of which are over water in the middle of the crossing. The story of this bridge, which is the reason for Maidenhead having been founded in the first place – in which case maybe it would have been more appropriate to have had reference to a bridge in the town's name rather than a reference to a maiden – is the story of a wooden bridge back in the 13th century that became a stone bridge in 1777 and a very controversial toll-free stone bridge in 1903. It is one of many stone bridges in the Thames Valley, built before nearby stone bridges across the river at Henley-on-Thames built in 1895, Windsor in 1824 and Marlow in 1832, but after a very small brick bridge at Sonning Village in 1775.

Although a small riverside village with a tiny population, Sonning has never been inconspicuous in the countryside around Maidenhead, not only because it is so picturesque – not infrequently likened to a village in the South of France (if one forgets the weather!) – but because, as William Camden reminds us in his *Britannia*, 'the little village of Sunning, which you would be surprised to think…was once the seat of eight bishops, who presided over this county [Berkshire] and Wilts. It [the seat of the bishops] was afterwards removed…to Salisbury'.

One would indeed be surprised to think such a thing, because Sonning is a mere speck of a village compared with a town the size of Salisbury – or compared with nearby Maidenhead – yet no less than eight bishops made their seat in this riverside village 'in beautiful meads', as Camden put it, and this is perhaps not so surprising since Sonning is by far one of the most beautiful and desirable locations between Maidenhead and Reading.

Sonning has always been near enough to Reading to become a residential retreat for the wealthy, a fashionable haunt that benefitted from two luxury hotels on either side of the Thames facing one another – the French Horn on one side and the White Hart on the other. It was, once upon a time, a popular place for boating, boat building and regattas, as I know from my own Berkshire roots having been born and brought up in Reading, not more than eight miles from Maidenhead and just a couple of miles down the road from Sonning Village, where I had a grandfather – John Henry Cole – who was a boat builder for the White Hart Hotel in Sonning village that was patronised by the rich and famous down from London, including the 20th-century music-hall singer and film star Gracie Fields, who came down from London to spend weekends at Sonning where she got to know my grandfather well. Even the notorious early 18th-century highwayman Dick Turpin is supposed to have been able to afford his own cottage in Sonning village, where there is a residence named after him to this day. Turpin would doubtless have been involved with the notorious gangs at Maidenhead Thicket – a beautiful spot for picnickers when I was a young man in the 1950s – who terrorised and attacked travellers in and out of Maidenhead in olden days, and it was he who made his legendary journey on his horse Black Bess from London to York, where he was finally hanged (the Turpin legend was popularised in Harrison Ainsworth's novel *Rockwood* in 1834).

Throughout the history of Maidenhead there are references made to a notorious gang of highwaymen and robbers who are supposed to have made Maidenhead Thicket a no-go area in the days of horse-drawn coaches – who had no choice but to pass it – and it is inconceivable that an enterprising highwayman like Dick Turpin would not have wanted a slice of the action, so Sonning village would have been a discreetly convenient and highly respectable hole in the wall for him (when I was a young man Maidenhead Thicket was safe enough – 'courting country', where couples got intimate behind bushes and in the long grass beyond the public view).

So it would not have been surprising if little Sonning had stolen a modest march on Maidenhead with a small brick bridge of its own back in 1775, for it too was already a place of some importance and indeed wealth. But Maidenhead's much larger 1777 stone bridge was way ahead of an iron bridge at Cookham in 1867, and stone bridges at Reading in 1923 and Caversham in 1926. The history of the Thames Valley is one of wooden river bridges being replaced by brick, iron and stone versions all the way from Windsor and Maidenhead, right up river to the university city of Oxford. First came the wooden bridges, to be followed by other bridges, and then to be joined in some cases by the railway bridges in the fullness of time, and from this meandering river most of the local history has flowed, as has national and international history out of London and the Thames Estuary, where the Thames Valley ends, flowing into the oceans and four corners of the earth. Let us not forget that when King John went to sign the Magna Carta at Runnymede near Egham on the south bank of the River Thames – as a statement of civil rights and curtailment of royal power in 1215 – he stayed at Sonning en route, in a Bishop's Palace there. Original copies of this all-important document can be found in the magnificent British Library at Euston in North London to this day, as well as in the ancient cathedrals of Salisbury and Lincoln.

One of the recurring problems for Maidenhead throughout its history is that, notwithstanding its startling enterprise, a number of nearby places have stolen a march on it and overshadowed it. Maidenhead used to have its own racecourse attended by royals, but it doesn't anymore, and it is to Royal Ascot that people flock from London, all over Berkshire (as my father and grandfather did on so many occasions) and other parts of the country. Maidenhead started off as the gateway to the Thames, with scenic Bolter's Lock, yet it lost out to nearby Henley-on-Thames and Marlow for picturesque and colourful regattas, and especially to the former town for rowing. Maidenhead started life with a great many country inns and hotels, yet, with the demise of Skindle's riverside hotel in the 20th century, it is no longer a haunt for fashionable and luxury hotels. In fact, the town centre of Maidenhead is now a mish-mash of tacky modernity, not a pleasant sight.

Some people take the view that although the railways put Maidenhead on the map for a second time in its history they killed off the river traffic and the boating, which went to nearby Henley, Marlow and Sonning instead (none of which were big railway centres), when travelling people took to the trains and forgot about the boats, and then in due course it lost out to Reading as a big railway junction, cattle market and agricultural centre (just as it had lost out to Reading previously for aforementioned reasons). And with Windsor's royal attractions, Maidenhead was always going to lose out to that town. *The Companion into Berkshire* tells us that 'Henley forestalled Maidenhead' as the chief centre for boating and rowing because the first Oxford and Cambridge boat race, in 1829, and also another in 1837, were 'held from Hambledon Lock to Henley'.

Whatever the reasons, Maidenhead fell behind these other places nearby, and if readers or local historians have any explanations as to why I shall be interested to hear from them. Maidenhead enjoyed a brief period of fashion when it was much more of a scenic river town than it managed to remain, when Eton schoolboys and their parents came down to the highly-fashionable Skindle's hotel in the earlier part of the 20th century – as did Guards officers and the cream of London society for their naughty weekends – but it was relatively short-lived. Probably its most fashionable and successful period in history is back in the days of the coaching inns, when it definitely stole a march on Bray and Cookham and got ahead of Windsor and Reading in becoming the first and last stop transport town outside London. When the railways came and cut the time it took to get from London to Maidenhead, no longer a full day by horse-drawn coaches, this first and last stop factor became increasingly irrelevant, so, ironically, what had made Maidenhead in the first place was now being killed off. Sure, the railways would bring a bigger population and the relocation of offices and factories to Maidenhead, but the overnight coaching-inn business would go, as would the blacksmithing, vetting and weekending (on faster trains people could get to many other places further afield in the time that it had taken to get to Maidenhead by road).

Interestingly, the stone bridge at Windsor – just down the road from Maidenhead – became toll free in 1897 ahead of Maidenhead in 1903, after Windsor people protested against the tolls, so it would seem that Maidenhead took a page out of Windsor's book in this regard. While Maidenhead got a bridge before Windsor, it also paid its tolls longer than its more rebellious neighbours, and the impetus to challenge and defy the tolls in Maidenhead came from a resident of Eton/Windsor, not Maidenhead.

Near to Taylor's bridge is Boulter's Lock, half in Maidenhead and half out of it, which has long been heralded as the picturesque gateway to and impulse of the 'River of Pleasure', with a staggering 1,400 large and small crafts – barges as well as pleasure boats – going through the lock daily at the height of the season during the 20th century. Pleasure seekers far and wide have been attracted to Boulter's Lock, which, in its hey day, has vied with Henley-on-Thames and its famous regatta as a fashionable star attraction. As a centre for up-river traffic, it takes its name not from a Mr Boulter, as one might suppose, but from the word boulter, which referred, once upon a time, to a miller. With a riverside water mill at the lock for the grinding and milling (called boulting) of corn, the lock soon took its name from this, although the spelling of the name today suggests that it may have belonged to a Mr Boulter, but that is not the case. It was a miller's lock, a place where a mill was conveniently located to grind corn and ship it up and down river. Next to the mill stood a brewery – Bell's Brewery – which was eventually taken over by Fuller's Brewery before becoming a hotel called the Bell Hotel. As we can see, this stone bridge that spanned the river at Maidenhead was essential to its prosperity, just like the wooden bridge before it. The bridge was prime property and the lock was key to the success of the river traffic on which so much depended.

Near to Boulter's Lock is Taplow Court, a stately home where the mayors of Maidenhead have entertained visiting royalty and where Saxon remains have been found and removed to the British Museum for safekeeping, since there is no history museum in Maidenhead.

The magnificent Cliveden is also nearby – an even greater stately home, currently a luxury hotel – with its classic grounds of landscaped parkland and gardens, its woodland and views over the river, its own boathouse, its stunning Italianate palace and its Joan of Arc and Prince Albert statues.

Popular with American millionaires, Cliveden was once the home of the former 'fabulous Astors', in early 20th-century days when Lord Astor owned *The Observer* newspaper and when his American wife, Lady Astor, became the first woman MP to sit in the House of Commons, championing women's rights and education and inheriting her husband's former constituency.

Cliveden has been owned by several titled people in its time, including a duchess. It was once the home of the Earl of Orkney, a famous 18th-century general and field marshal in the Duke of Marlborough's service – he of Blenheim Palace and the Churchill family – and the Orkney Arms in Maidenhead was named after him. It was in Cliveden that the so-called 'Cliveden set' was formed in the early 1900s when a handpicked assembly of some 23–30 frightfully wealthy and influential individuals, all highly educated, well groomed and well connected – and most out of South Africa following the Boer War – regularly met at Cliveden to form a quasi secret society of their own that was intended to influence the British government of the day, pulling strings behind the scenes and manipulating its policies. This was according to Claude Cockburn, founder and editor of *The Week*, who coined the term 'the Cliveden Set' in 1937, accusing it of being a bunch of wealthy aristocrats who wanted to do a deal with Hitler rather than go to war with him, as Winston Churchill had every intention of doing and as doubtless the Earl of Orkney and the Duke of Marlborough would have done in the days when the earl lived in Cliveden.

Again, we can see how closely related to national and international events Maidenhead has been. When the scandalous 'Profumo affair' hit the headlines in the 1960s, revealing how parties for toffs and MPs down from London had been held at Cliveden with nude prostitutes and skinny dipping in the pool – notably Christine Keeler and the Tory cabinet minister John Profumo – Cliveden and Maidenhead were in the national consciousness yet again, albeit for the wrong reasons!

Much better were the headlines concerning Sir Robert Taylor's stone bridge and Isambard Brunel's remarkable railway bridge, as we shall see in the following chapter.

CHAPTER EIGHT

The Coming of the Railways to Victorian Maidenhead

Although the history of Maidenhead is essentially the story of a river and a bridge for the first 257 years of its life – from 1582 when Queen Elizabeth I granted Maidenhead its township status until 1839 when the first Great Western railway line and regular trains came to the town – thereafter this history becomes a very different story indeed, and it is even more startling than the first story that has been told in the first seven chapters of this book.

This time it's the story of a railway line and its steam trains. And this second story is the story of the greatest and most original engineer and inventor in England to leave his mark on Maidenhead.

It was Isambard Brunel who not only built the Great Western Railways between London's Paddington Station and Bristol, but also built Maidenhead's first and last railway bridge, and this is the story of the difference that he and the Great Western Railways made to Maidenhead. No sooner had the first trains arrived in Maidenhead than some 10,000 people a week were travelling between the capital city and the small country town, which was poised for much more rapid growth than hitherto. This really was breathtaking history – the whole of Maidenhead and the Thames Valley was buzzing with excited talk about the railways and where they might go next. The novelist Charles Dickens was no less excited, writing them into his novels as and when appropriate.

All around London, small towns would become larger as a result of the railways that would reach out to them, and people were learning how to commute, how to live in one place and work in another, how to trade much more by sending their wares and their fresh country produce and cattle by rail, how to escape from the capital city at weekends to enjoy the country air, how to live in the big city but have a house in the country, how to go and live permanently in the country, how to travel and get to know people in other parts of the country of whom they may have heard but who were foreign to them because they had not previously visited their towns and cities, how to invest in all sorts of ways at the end of the line. A small London bookseller and newsagent called W.H.Smith became a national chain by following the railways all over the country and opening a shop at each station, having opened its first station shop at Euston in North London. This family became seriously rich and socially elevated in no time at all and finished up buying a country house overlooking the Thames outside Henley, which later became the home of the Henley Management College. What the railways brought to Maidenhead and the rest of the country was an entirely new, unimaginable and unprecedented kind of history, thanks to the invention of the steam train and the investment that was pouring into the railways. It was by far the most important element in Maidenhead's history.

Other elements in Maidenhead's history prior to the arrival of the Great Western Railways – already mentioned in passing in this book – included: the history of the local church in Maidenhead; the history of coaching inns and breweries; and the history of horse-drawn traffic between London in the east and Bristol in the west. These are all mentioned only in passing because they do not constitute the essential driving force in the greater history of Maidenhead, which was the river, the bridge and the Pinkney's Green/Elentone pioneers, without whom there would have been no town with its coaching inns, breweries, mayors, priests and churches. Everything has risen up out of the river and around its banks and then around the London road, making its way westward to Bristol and Bath.

But there are other minor histories to be told about the town of Maidenhead, the copious details of which are not to be found in these pages because, as I say, they strike me as being relatively minor (local historians and history teachers may feel free to disagree).

Where the history of the local church in Maidenhead is concerned, this was the history of the beginning of civic life in Maidenhead with the founding of the Guild of St Andrew and St Mary Magdalene in December 1451, which had been responsible for the maintenance of the town's wooden bridge over the river and its chapel. As we have seen, this wooden bridge and the stone one that followed it were key to the town's prominence and prosperity, and the church played its part in this, as did the guild of tradesmen and craftsmen, of which today's borough council is a direct descendant. This was the pattern all over the country, and Maidenhead was no exception. There are so many minor histories within minor histories in Maidenhead's religious communities, with their Catholic, Church of England, Congregational, Baptist, Weslyn Methodist and Society of Friends congregations, and with other denominations besides, all of which have left their mark on the town, as have Maidenhead's different mayors, schools, charities, courts, local institutions and town hall. But this is a history that looks at the local history of Maidenhead from a bigger and broader point of view, to see where it fits into the national scheme of things and see what has made it what it is today.

Thus far, Maidenhead has touched national history by providing that first essential stepping stone out of London into the near west of England and beyond, making its all-important contribution to a network of horse-drawn transportation that put the west of England in touch with the capital city, and the capital city in touch with the west of England. Maidenhead has facilitated the necessary travel of people between east and west, the transportation of goods and fresh country produce between east and west, as has every town along the east-west route of course, but Maidenhead was the first and last of those towns, depending on which way one's cargoes were travelling. Once the connection had been made from London to Maidenhead, then further connections could be added, as indeed they were. And within Berkshire and the Thames Valley, Maidenhead has contributed to the growth and prosperity of the region – as have all the other major towns – by turning itself into something from nothing and providing a centre of trade and commerce, originally for farmers but thereafter for all sorts. Had it not managed to do this, it may very well have remained an inconspicuous suburb of Bray and Cookham – a no man's land in between – rather than having overshadowed those delightful places and forged ahead.

In the same way that the wooden bridge over the river brought prosperity to Maidenhead, so too did the Great Western Railways, and on a far bigger scale. The *Piggott's Gazetteer* referred to the coming of the railways in England as a 'stupendous undertaking and rapid mode of transit', as one can well imagine that it must have been on 30 May 1838 when the first experimental train journey found its way into Maidenhead.

It wasn't until the following year that non-experimental trains regularly visited Maidenhead, in 1839, which is the date used in these pages for the advent of of the railways in Maidenhead. Queen Victoria's first train journey was from Slough to London Paddington in 1842 when she said that she was 'charmed by it'.

It took the first trains more than one hour to make the journey from London – previously it had taken horses one day – for which a new railway station had been built and opened to the public at Taplow on 4 June. We are told that this station was located opposite an inn called the Dumb Bell, and it was constructed in a 'most primitive order of architecture' for a railway station. It was located one-and-three-quarter miles from the town because the railway bridge over the river was not ready on time and so the trains stopped outside, but not before a telegraph station and signal box had been put in at the village of Slough (hard to imagine when we visit that light industrial estate and former 'new town' today).

There were two trains – the *Vulcan* and the *Northern Star* – with first and second-class coaches and an open wagon at the back for third-class passengers. Eton College near Windsor was chartering special trains for the transportation of its pupils who henceforth came to their posh public boarding school via Maidenhead, just as the parents of those pupils often wined and dined in Maidenhead when they visited them. Clearly, Maidenhead was in the national spotlight because of its geographical gateway position west of London – due to its road bridge across the river that had attracted a railway bridge in its wake.

The first rail journeys were without doubt uncomfortable – a bumpy ride in poorly-sprung coaches over uneven track – but it did not matter, the GWR show was on the road, and people were throwing their hats in the air as Maidenhead had been put on the map once again. The first 24 miles of track between London's Paddington Station and Maidenhead's Taplow Station – with other stations soon to follow in the town of Maidenhead – was tremendously symbolic because more than another 9,000 miles of GWR track depended on the success or otherwise of this first 24 miles. Maidenhead was in the public eye nationally and also regionally as businesses and other people in Bristol and Bath waited impatiently for the trains to get clear of Maidenhead and reach them, and people in Reading and Swindon waited likewise for the next step of the journey to be completed. Not that it would be easy, because there were no mechanical excavators or power shovels in those days – everything was reliant on manual labour and the sweat of a workman's brow – and there was a hill approaching Sonning that stood in the way, and two miles of cutting to be carved out of high ground between Twyford and Reading.

However, for the train to reach the station a new railway bridge was required across the river – like the wooden and stone bridges before it – and this bridge, unlike the railway station, was anything but primitive, constructed by the great Isambard Brunel. Wesley tells us it was a 'remarkable as well as a graceful structure' at a cost of £37,000 in 1837–39, almost twice the cost of Sir Robert Taylor's stone bridge (still standing in Maidenhead today, as is the railway bridge) at £19,000 back in the 18th century. This railway bridge was reckoned to be the largest and most remarkable span of brickwork in the country. It has brick arches across the river, which were the widest and flattest in the world when first constructed in Maidenhead, changing its identity from a coach and horses town to a graceful railway town (no sheds and engineering works here – they went to Swindon, halfway between London and Bristol – this was Maidenhead, after all!)

Without doubt the most important men in the history of Maidenhead – since the original unknowns from Pinkney's Green/South Ellington and Elentone – have been an architect and an engineer. Sir Robert Taylor, who architected the stone bridge, made all the difference to the prosperity and amenity of the town and its future prospects, as did Isambard Brunel, whose remarkable railway bridge across the river in Maidenhead made an even bigger difference in the fullness of time.

These two men and their unknown bridge-building predecessors, presumably carpenters, stand head and shoulders above the rest – above the bishops, the chaplains and priests, the innkeepers, the blacksmiths and stable keepers, the vets and doctors, the stonemasons and farmers in the surrounding countryside, and even above the monarchs who gave the permission for Maidenhead to become a town and for the trees to be taken from their estates to help repair that all-important first river bridge, none of whom would have had any reason to come to Maidenhead in the first place or to have a continuing interest in this village that turned itself into a town had it not been for these wooden, stone and brickwork bridge builders, with their carpentry, architectural and engineering skills.

Of course, those who built the roads, hospitals, offices and houses and shifted sewage are all of equal importance, but without the vision and expertise of Messrs Taylor and Brunel and the wooden bridge builders there would have been no reason to build a town or to deal with its sewage, and that is the point that we need to grasp about this period in Maidenhead's history, which has been driven by river bridges, boats and trains more than anything else.

There is in the centre of Maidenhead – in King Street – an excellent modern sculpture of an innocent-looking and handsome young boy holding a sailing boat. But one feels that the poor lad is rather lost, surrounded as he is by a fair amount of tat in a modern, cramped and rather scruffy shopping precinct, where there is no idyllic suggestion of a graceful river nearby, or even of a park with a pond for his boat. One feels that this sculpture is too gentle, stylish and elegant for a goodly number of the shops that surround it, as shoppers and others rush by, hardly giving this boy or the subject of sailing a second thought (although, sadly, a local drunk has thought about him, having knocked the sculpture from its plinth on one occasion!).

One feels that this Maidenhead Boy derserves rather better than this, that he would be more comfortably and appropriately located near to the river or the handsome stone bridge that crosses it. On the other hand, here he is in the thick of it, plucky young lad, in the rough and tumble of everyday living, brushing shoulders with all sorts, where he can be seen by many more people to remind them of their riverside heritage and boating history, not that they have much time for such thoughts as they rush to and from their local shops, offices and pubs. This boy is also an unwitting reminder of how the graceful image of Maidenhead has dramatically declined in recent decades. His sculpture demonstrates the difficulty of reflecting local history in art and making it relevant to the public at large in today's world, and this brings us to the subject of our next chapter about art, statues and local history.

CHAPTER NINE

Art and Local History

We have seen, in the previous chapter, how the local history of the railways coming to Maidenhead brought England's greatest engineer of the 19th century to the town in order to construct a railway bridge across the Thames.

But it also brought England's greatest artist of that era.

William Turner came from London to paint one of the first trains crossing Brunel's famous bridge at Maidenhead, and by so doing he put what was still a small country town on the nation's cultural map, just as Brunel had put it on the geographical and technological map. Again, the connection between local and national history is inescapable, as we see how Maidenhead was put not only in the national consciousness of art lovers who frequented national art galleries – and of those who practised, studied and taught art, whether locally or nationally – but of railway and engineering people likewise. To this day, art lovers, who have never been to Maidenhead in their lives, know Turner's painting of Maidenhead Bridge.

So a double whammy for Maidenhead once upon a time!

Not until 1957 would the town record another double whammy, when, during that year, two events of national importance took place in Maidenhead: the world's first vertical take-off aircraft flight (a Fairey Rotodyne), which was of international as well as national significance, and the production in the town of the first British car (a Vanwall) to win a British Grand Prix since 1934, driven by Stirling Moss.

Turner's famous painting of a train crossing Maidenhead's railway bridge is called *Rain, Steam and Speed – The Great Western Railway*; it hangs in London's National Gallery today and is well worth a visit. The artist gives us a painting of a dimly perceived bridge – as, indeed, the first trains and railways bridges were dimly perceived by the general public that was still horse-drawn at that time – depicting a very fiery steam train crossing Brunel's very famous bridge, as that bridge and the train then get lost in sheets of rain that are lashing from all directions.

This is not a clearly-defined railway bridge or train, but a suitably impressionistic one that is laden with symbolism.

The painting can be perceived as a symbol of how man rises to the eternal challenge of the elements to make the progress that he must make – without really knowing what lies ahead for his new inventions – and also of how Brunel and his railway bridge rise to the challenge likewise, as the new and revolutionary bridge (at that time) stands firm in the struggle that is going on between the rain and the steam.

Golden rain and golden steam glistening in the fiery yet misty light of the heavens render the outward shape and form of the bridge barely visible, but visible enough for viewers to understand what is going on in the painting, as the town of Maidenhead becomes a blur in the background.

And what is going on in the painting – as in so many of Turner's landscapes – is a titanic struggle between nature, on the one hand, and locomotive engineering, bridge building and human enterprise on the other, both pitting themselves against each other.

Mother Nature sends her wind and rain to come crashing down on early 19th-century railway locomotion and bridge building in Maidenhead, at a time in British history when people were unaccustomed to heavy trains – loaded with cargoes and passengers – crossing railway bridges, and when steam trains were coming out of a dimly perceived world of mysterious technology and engineering, changing the face of the map and society forever.

For those with the eyes to see all this, there is a clear unity in this painting, which is actually quite a clever and thought-provoking work of art presented atmospherically as well as impressionistically by Turner, who was well known for painting natural tragedy in natural landscape. This was something that was deeply ingrained in his psyche. In this sense he was also interested in natural philosophy, reminding people of how awesome and tragic nature is, with all its destructive effects and monstrous storms at sea and killer waves, giant mountains rising up like gods through frozen and impenetrable – untouchable – landscapes, all of which can be, and frequently are, very tragic. But his paintings also showed the hope and triumph of man over adversity and the constant struggle of men to this end.

But there is nothing tragic about *Rain, Steam and Speed*. There is, rather, a sense in which man has got nature on the run at last, but not without a struggle, as the powerful train, spitting fire and puffing great clouds of steam, bursts through the wind and rain that is clouding its vision and standing in its path. This train crossing Maidenhead Bridge had catapulted Turner's obsession with the past into the future and pointed him in a new direction, which is exactly what the arrival of the railways and Brunel's amazing (at that time) railway bridge had done to the town of Maidenhead.

But there is also a sense here of how a painting can demonstrate the important difference that art makes to local history – and, by the same token, that local history makes to art – and the difference that both make to our national history and heritage.

Yet again, the link between local and national history is of significance here.

It was hardly surprising that Turner was interested in the coming of the railways. He was a tireless traveller who not only visited many parts of Britain during the 1790s but also travelled to France, Switzerland, Holland and Germany from about 1802–19, before the advent of the railways in 1825 when the world's first public rail service opened between Stockton and Darlington and then with Stephenson's *Rocket* ahead of the service that reached Maidenhead in 1839. But Stephenson's *Rocket*, in 1829, was a long way behind the inventions of the first steam engines in Britain by Newcomen in 1712 – pumping water out of mines – and Trevithick in his Cornish tin mine in 1804, with the first engine to run on tracks underground, and the first to carry passengers in 1801. Stephenson's *Rocket*, on the new Liverpool–Manchester line, came almost three decades after Trevithick.

Without doubt, the railways were an exclusively British preserve, with the expertise and the enterprise happening in Britain ahead of the rest of the world.

Reportedly, not until 1842 did the United States of America get a railway – between Boston and Albany – using British locomotives and rails because the Americans had neither the expertise nor the vehicles and equipment. They were quick to purchase it and then to learn how to do it for themselves, but they were not in a position to do it themselves to begin with. Nor were most of the Europeans. The successful arrival of the first train in Maidenhead – without mishap or set back – was good news, not only for England as a whole but for the Americans likewise, since they were keen to follow suit.

Once again we see the connection between local, national and international history, but there is also a regional connection because what happened in Maidenhead at the local level was as a result of what had happened in a region of the North of England, just as what happened regionally throughout the entire region of the south west of England happened as a result of what was going on locally in Maidenhead to begin with, where the success of the first service between London to Maidenhead was not just a local event but a truly national one – with regional implications – with the capital city reaching out into Berkshire and beyond.

What was happening locally and regionally was soon to influence what would happen internationally, not just in the US but throughout the rest of Europe, including the Soviet Union. Maidenhead really was at the centre of these early pioneering developments, which is why the eyes of the world were on this quiet country town as the world watched what was going on with railway locomotion in Britain. Had the Maidenhead bit of the broader national and international picture not worked, then there would have been a serious set back for rail travel regionally, nationally and internationally. As it was, it worked very well, and it was all this national and international significance that the artist William Turner was capturing in his famous painting that he came to Maidenhead to paint, an historical painting that was of interest to people in more ways than one – in more ways than usual.

Even towards the end of his life, Turner was still the dedicated traveller, who made repeated excursions to Venice and Switzerland, and he also did a tour of Normandy in 1845. So one can well imagine his enthusiasm for Maidenhead's first railway bridge in 1838, when it was designed and engineered by the famous Brunel and became the biggest brickwork construction in the country (not that you would guess this from Turner's depiction of it).

The excitement in those days must have been electric!

One can also imagine people doing a hop, skip and a jump from London to Maidenhead – a mere 24 miles away by rail – to take a look at this famous bridge, and one can just see the famous painter snatching his easel and his paints and rushing to Maidenhead with an eye for a new and futuristic subject to paint. Usually Turner painted seascapes, ships, coastal scenes, mountains, rivers and lakes – as well as apocalyptic, mythical and historical paintings – all with a very modern approach to light and luminosity, and many great paintings of his were, and still are, bursting with atmosphere.

So near at hand, Maidenhead Railway Bridge was made for such an artist, who was sometimes romantic in his approach, other times epic, and always with a keen eye for light in landscape. His astonishing capacity to evoke the nuances of natural and artificial light was well employed in his painting of Maidenhead's railway bridge, and his interest in history – ever present in so many of his paintings – would have driven him in the direction of Isambard Brunel and his truly historic bridge.

Because Turner was also interested in mythology and natural philosophy, it is perhaps hardly surprising that there is a touch of the mythological in the fire-eating monster of his train as it crosses the bridge and the river at Maidenhead, the same river that had been crossed by Danish Viking invaders centuries before when, as we have seen, King Alfred fought the Danes – albeit without any troop trains with which to send his soldiers to Maidenhead to apprehend the invaders.

There is an impressionistic intensity about Turner's train and bridge, which was a 'first' for the art world in those days, just as Brunel's actual bridge was a first for Maidenhead.

As for Brunel, he was the most original inventor of 19th-century Britain, just as Turner was the most original painter. He, too, would have been draw to Maidenhead like a magnet when he heard that a railway bridge was required there.

What a challenge!

And so conveniently near at hand and close to the capital city.

While his most famous works were yet to come for Brunel (The Clifton Suspension Bridge at Bristol in 1864 – a mighty bridge spanning the mighty Avon Gorge – and the world's first iron ship, the *Great Britain*, in 1843), the bridge at Maidenhead was nevertheless an important 'first' for Brunel and the country, if the 1600 kilometres of broad-gauge track (rather than the smaller standard gauge) was to reach out from London to Bristol and beyond.

For Brunel, Maidenhead Bridge was one of his earliest railway challenges and a vital stepping stone to what he was to achieve later at Clifton. His name – and that of the artist Turner – will always be associated with Maidenhead in the minds of those who know their history or their art history.

One wonders why Maidenhead has not made more of its connection with these men – both artists in their very different ways. The town is definitely missing a trick here, for this information is not only of interest to local historians and inhabitants alike, but to tourists as well. To have inspired Britain's greatest engineer and greatest painter of the 19th century is not an insignificant aspect of the town's history, yet it is not featured in any of the earlier histories of the town.

There is a happy harmony between art and engineering here, a meeting of both these opposite worlds – an example of art comprehending engineering – and exploring this, along with everything else, is an example of what local history at its best can and should be about (or so it seems to me), as local history discovers and gives prominence to previously unknown connections and things from past times that have not formally been realised or recognised.

This is what makes local history exciting and relevant in the modern world.

The modern world takes trains for granted, as it passes by rail through Maidenhead, but what does it know of the history and significance of rail and the difference it made to Maidenhead and to all Thames Valley towns, and what does it know of Turner having painted Maidenhead Bridge or of Brunel having engineered that bridge? If there were statues of Brunel and Turner at Maidenhead Station, the modern world would have more reason to realise these things.

The railways promoted the growth of new towns and existing old towns, while also relieving some of the coastal ports of their domestic freight, which could suddenly go by rail for internal distribution instead of round the coast as before. The railways also promoted the growth of villages, likewise, turning many of them into towns. Slough, near Maidenhead, is one such example, which went from sleepy village before the advent of modern rail to modern town and industrial estate thereafter.

The Thames Valley – and Reading in particular, because it became the railway capital of the region – really was opened up and put well and truly on the map by the railways, just as Maidenhead was put on the map by Turner's painting and Brunel's bridge.

Reading became the Crewe of the South (along with Swindon in Wiltshire to a lesser extent, with its railway repair sheds), or, in an international context, the Bowani Junction of the Thames Valley, as more and more trains from so many different directions connected at Reading, and more and more local people looked to the railways for jobs.

As a result of the railways, small towns came alive around London, with, typically, populations of some 10,000 people doubling in size on account of the railways, and places like Slough were no longer able to continue as sleepy little villages.

In particular, the railways made it possible for fresh food and milk to be conveyed swiftly from country to town and for householders everywhere to get their hands on coal with which to heat and fuel their previously cold and damp houses – millions of tons of coal!

And with more people able to travel from town to town they got to know their fellow countrymen and women better, and became less suspicious of them. People in different regions were better able to understand each other thanks to the railways, and to become less insular in the process. They could escape from their own communities and go elsewhere, and appreciate other communities and the way they did things.

The first trains travelled at not more than about 30–36mph, and this was considered to be swift indeed, so the social progress and economic growth that they brought about was, by that yardstick, no less swift.

The railways were to Maidenhead what the wooden bridge across the river had been to the town previously. When the trains were first introduced, the public were always trying to board them illegally and get a free ride. Just like natives in India to this day – and there's another international connection to be made here – people in and around Maidenhead (and throughout the rest of England) sat on the roof tops of carriages and clung to the sides of wagons, jumping on and off trains to dodge the ticket collectors.

There were 15 times as many passenger accidents in unruly Britain back then as there were in Germany, and this was for the simple reason that the Germans introduced affordable third-class carriages for their passengers, whereas the British did not get round to this until 1844 when the free-riding poor were provided with a safe and secure means of travel.

Not only did the railways spur the growth of villages, towns and cities, but of national business developments likewise. We have already seen how W.H.Smith, the bookseller and newsagent, opened its first railway bookshop at Euston Station in North London and proceeded to mushroom from there into a national chain, with bookstalls at each railway station countrywide, totalling around 200.

So Maidenhead – thanks to the railways – had arrived in the modern world (just as it had arrived in the previous modern world before that, thanks to horse-drawn coaches), but what kind of history has it had in the modern world?

Its modern history is no less startling, as we shall see from the following chapter in this book.

––––––––––––––––––––

CHAPTER TEN

Maidenhead in Modern Times

When one looks at the history of Maidenhead in the modern world, say from the late 19th and early 20th centuries, it continues to startle, and not least on account of two massive floods that were startling for the wrong reasons – the first in 1894 (claimed by the Maidenhead Heritage Centre as the greatest flood on record) and another in 1947 (also claimed as the most severe flood of the 20th century) – because of which an even more startling man-made river has been built as part of a Flood Alleviation Scheme, a river that is the biggest of its kind in Britain and the second biggest in Europe.

Maidenhead's vulnerability to flooding is a real problem for the town on account of its nearness to the river and its low-lying areas and wetlands, which is why, in the new millennium, the Maidenhead Windsor & Eton Flood Alleviation Scheme – known locally as the Jubilee River – was introduced in 2002 in order to provide protection against floods of the magnitude of 1947 and of 1894.

It was called the Jubilee River to mark Queen Elizabeth II's Golden Jubilee Year in 2002, and it provides an hydraulic channel for Maidenhead, Windsor and Eton that is some 11.6 kilometres long, taking any overflow from the River Thames that may result from floods in future years. Because it is man-made it has the capacity to control the waters so that it cannot flood, while it takes the excess from an overflowing Thames. This is a highly complex civil-engineering achievement by any standard, of national and international interest, which is well known to the people of Maidenhead but not to a great many people elsewhere in the country or in Europe.

While Maidenhead's 1947 flood was estimated to be 10 to 20cms lower than that of 1894, it was nevertheless devastating, flooding 2,000 homes. The same floods today would, the experts say, affect 5,500 homes and 12,500 people, damaging roads, railways, businesses and vital services, including gas, electricity and telephones.

While there are many advantages to living in the beautiful Thames Valley, flooding is not one of them. It is the downside of an otherwise beautifully lush and scenic environment, and, while Windsor may very well be the Queen of England's preferred residence outside London, flooding has a nasty habit of upsetting royal as well as everybody else's applecarts, but she is now equally as well protected as her subjects by this flood alleviation scheme.

At a cost £83.5 million, it took some 20 years to complete this scheme after all the engineering, technical, ecological and social problems – including the compulsory purchase orders – had been thrashed out, with local community involvement, of course. The history of this man-made river is a vast subject and a story in itself (worthy of another local history book perhaps), but, to cut a very long and complicated story short, what the river does is this: it takes the flood waters away from residential properties and homes – as well as local businesses – and re-circulates them in its own good time.

Sheer magic (at least in theory!)

This achievement of the Jubilee River is of the same magnitude as any of the accomplishments of Maidenhead's past. However, there is an important difference: it is not a purely Maidenhead community enterprise. On the contrary, it is a shared enterprise with nearby Windsor and Eton (reminding us of the important regional connections in any local history). But, then again, Brunel's railway bridge, that was an enterprise between a London railway company and an engineer of national celebrity, and the local community that employed him. All of which surely goes to prove – does it not? – the importance of national and international connections to local history (no man – no community – is an island). And like the GWR railway exercise back in the 19th century, which was of interest to the outside world because the outside world had things to learn from it to its advantage. So the Jubilee River has lessons for the outside world in its efforts to cope with the increasing incidence of flooding these days. As we see, one thing connects to another and another, as do countries and local communities in different periods of time.

Since the coaching era of Maidenhead started to come to an end in 1839 – when the railways and Brunel's famous bridge began to seriously startle, and then when the toll on Maidenhead's stone bridge was lifted in 1903, followed by the advent of motor cars for those who could afford them – the town has witnessed other startling events in its history, including the manufacture of the aforementioned Vanwall racing car, and the world's first successful flight of a vertical take-off aircraft, both in the 1950s.

Halfway through the 20th century, Maidenhead was continuing to startle as it had previously and from the very beginning. It had started the century with four Victoria Crosses being awarded to local people during World War One (1914–18) when the town's population of 13,000 people suffered 900 casualties, and by the time of World War Two in 1939 Britain's wartime headquarters of the Air Transport Auxiliary was established at White Waltham aerodrome after it had been opened in 1935.

One of the difficulties for local historians researching and writing the local history of towns such as Maidenhead in modern times – since the 1960s – is that times are not as localised in their community developments and histories as they used to be. Their inhabitants are no longer local people, necessarily, with deep roots in the town for generations. This is because there has been a breakdown in the local community structure. There was a time when families in towns and cities throughout Britain lived in the same streets and neighbourhoods for decades, maybe even centuries, without moving away. They stayed put and made much more local history as a result, living and dying where they were born.

For more than a century after the coming of the railways in 1839, most local people in Maidenhead and elsewhere remained local and firmly settled in their communities, with their parents, grandparents, uncles and aunts all living nearby and meeting weekly or fortnightly. Of course, they visited other towns and cities from time to time – thanks to the railways – but most people seldom if ever became residents of those places. By staying put, they knew each other well and who was related to whom, and they carried their local history round in their heads, as it had been told to them by their parents, grandparents, uncles and aunts, to whom it had been told by their parents, grandparents, uncles and aunts in turn. Everybody knew everybody else's business and, in a great many cases, people worked for the same employers for generations, as did their children and their children's children.

Communities were therefore very tight-knit. But all this went after World War Two – from the 1950s and 1960s – when there was a great sea change in local communities throughout the country, and not least in Maidenhead, of course.

This was a sea change that was welcomed by those who found their tight-knit communities too stifling, but not by those who liked having the certainty and the strong arms of a local community around them, such as my parents, grandparents, uncles and aunts in Reading.

There was a tribal sense of 'our street', 'our neighbourhood' and 'our town', but this sense of a purely local community and its community spirit and structure no longer exists today in towns such as Reading or Maidenhead, and most others for that matter.

There was also a sense of nationhood and empire, once upon a time, that was alive and well in the history of Maidenhead, as we know from Wesley Walker, who tells us that an Empire Day was inaugurated in Maidenhead in 1905 by the then mayor, Mr B. Hobbs. These Empire Days existed all over the UK until as recently as the 1950s, as I recall from my own childhood in Reading when school children attended these events, parading the streets, dressed in the uniforms and costumes of different countries of the British Empire (I remember my mother dressing me up as a Canadian Mounted Policeman!). They were held on 24 May, Queen Victoria's birthday, but were changed to Commonwealth Days in 1958.

But with the loss of Empire and a goodly number of other things besides – and, more importantly, with the loss of local communities and the breakdown of community structures – local history is very far from being what it used to be, because without a permanently-based local community in the traditional sense, with its deep roots and spreading branches, it is hard to see where the history is going to come from in future times or what shape it is likely to take, shaped as it is by its own efforts and influenced as it is by national events that impact upon it. Without doubt, the faces of local history and of local communities are changing radically.

This is the biggest change in the history of local communities of the last half century, and it is a change that makes it difficult to get to grips with local history during this period, because much of it has become, in fact, no longer purely local, and it is important for researchers and writers of local history to be aware of this.

As more and more local people go to live elsewhere, towns and cities and their communities are losing and have lost their distinctive local and regional identities and differences.

So the local 'flavour' of most communities has gone.

What brought about this sea change in local communities and their histories was greatly improved (and much more affordable) transport between towns and cities everywhere, which made it so much easier for people from one part of the country to go and live and work in another part, and for business investors to go and invest in another and create jobs there.

Suddenly, local communities were set free, as it were, as people were able to cut themselves off from their roots and their tribe and go elsewhere, if that's what it took to improve their incomes, and their lives. The economic power structure of regions changed, making it necessary in many cases for people to migrate elsewhere in search of work.

In this way towns and cities took on a different character completely, with a new style of community emerging in which nobody knew or cared who anybody was anymore, where they came from or who their neighbours really were, as they lived anonymously and almost invisibly among one another.

One could move elsewhere and live next door to people whose roots were a mystery because they were from elsewhere. There was no consciousness of local community or history anymore. One could move into a community without being aware of its recent or distant history because one was too busy with other things to do and with places to go, as the community spirit, the gossip and the spying on each other went out of the back door as the 'elsewhere people' – from a wide range of different communities in different parts of the country and the outside world – came in the front door.

So traditional local history, as we know it, is in danger of dying out.

Even so, efforts are still being made by enthusiasts such as the Maidenhead Heritage Centre to preserve the history and records of local churches, societies, institutions, schools and clubs etc. But it is no longer as easy at it was once upon a time, when, traditionally, people stayed put in their local communities and generated more things of historical note, and were more readily definable as local people responsible for local events, as were their parents, grandparents and great grandparents before them. But there are still things of historical significance happening in the new-style local communities (with their roots no longer purely or at all local) that have replaced the old-style communities, and when we look at Maidenhead we see that by far the most significant historical development during the last century is, without doubt, the creation of the Jubilee River, for reasons of survival rather than local history.

This is the river that saved the town from the worst floods that it had seen since 1947, when, in 2003, (the year that Maidenhead Library became a listed building) this river came to the rescue of the town and showed what it could do – while nearby Cookham and Hurley were not, alas, so lucky, for those communities suffered the devastating effects of severe flooding.

So it seems only fitting to end this book on the history of Maidenhead – which is essentially a river history of a riverside town – on the subject of the town's Jubilee River and the difference it is making in the new millennium, when there is so much more history to be made in and around Maidenhead in the years ahead.

The overriding history of Maidenhead is, from beginning to end, the history of transport in one form or another and the difference that it makes to towns that would not otherwise have amounted to anything very much, or perhaps have come into being at all. It is the history first of horse-drawn road transport, then of river transport and then of rail transport. It was early, pioneering developments in all these things that brought the town of Maidenhead into being and enabled it to go from strength to strength, from the time when the people of Elentone and Pinkney's Green transported themselves across the river in boats – in order to build a wooden bridge to transport even more people across the river by road – to join up with another very important road there that was capable of transporting people out of London on a direct westerly route to Bristol and Bath, given the provision of coaching inns along the way to make that feasible.

And just as the coming of railway transport and automobiles put an end to the horse-drawn transport that had made the town of Maidenhead possible in the first place, so the coming of air transport at London's Heathrow Airport, which is also close to Maidenhead, has enabled the town to prosper yet again by attracting all sorts of businesses and warehouses that need to be near to Britain's premier airport for export reasons.

Gone are the days of horse-drawn transport, and also of the great flood of river transport that existed once upon a time to carry grain and other cargoes up and down the Thames at Maidenhead. For example, the picturesque Boulter's Lock at Maidenhead used to be the gateway to the Thames – the so-called 'pulse of the river' – with hundreds of big and small river craft passing through it in a single day during the season. It was heavily trafficked with pleasure boats, cargo boats and barges. But those days are also no more. Boulter's Lock is no longer the important river centre it used to be.

These days it makes sense to be near to London's Heathrow Airport rather than a river. Boulter's Lock, as picturesque as ever, is not the river transport centre it used to be, just as Maidenhead as a junction for horse-drawn coaches is not the important centre that it used to be, and transport is no longer the dominant factor in the success of this town as once it was.

From here on it seems that momentous developments in transport will be less and less important to the future history of Maidenhead – since there are no more momentous developments of that kind that are either foreseeable or necessary these days – and it seems that the future story of

Maidenhead will be very different indeed, at least very different from the one told in the pages of this book.

And on that note, I bring the history of Maidenhead to a close, leaving readers to wonder about the way ahead as they ponder on what went before.

———————————————

CHAPTER ELEVEN

In Conclusion

So what conclusions can we draw from this startling little story of the key developments in the history of Maidenhead?

When Wesley Walker wrote his 1930s history of the town, he observed that its history had not been adequately recorded for hundreds of years, taking the view that the reason for this was that Maidenhead had not been 'privileged to play a more striking part in English history'. He suggested that, had it been so and done so, its 'life and growth would have been more fully recorded'. Yet, as he acknowledged, every town has its story, striking or otherwise, and, in my opinion, while the history of Maidenhead may not be very striking, it is certainly very startling and should therefore be presented as such. I also feel that another reason for Maidenhead's history not having been fully recorded in the past is, of course, because it has not had a proper museum. Why it has not had a proper museum – why the temporary museum that it had in the early 20th century disappeared – seems to be a complete mystery!

Clearly, there is more research to be done here. What is it that motivates and enables some towns more than others to get themselves a museum? Who made the decision not to go ahead with a museum and just stick with a public lending library instead? Why is it that some towns are more careless of their history than others? Who were Britain's great museum makers? Not just the big city museums, where the reasons for having a museum are more predictable and obvious, but the smaller museums in the smaller towns? Obviously, there is scope for another book here. Maybe the wise and the good of Maidenhead agreed with Wesley Walker that the town's history was not sufficiently 'striking' for it to justify a museum, but, as I hope that I have demonstrated in this book, there has in fact been enough going on for the town to have had its own museum.

Since the Wesley Walker history, there have been a handful of other latter-day histories, including Andrew Martin's *Maidenhead: A History and Celebration of the Town*, Tom Middleton's *Yesterday's Town: Maidenhead, The Story of this Place and the Men Who Made It*, and Luke Over's *The Story of Maidenhead*. There has also been Joy Dillaway's *Short History of Maidenhead: 5th to 13th Centuries* and *An Outline History of Maidenhead* by the local Heritage Centre, none of which I have researched for my book because I wanted to go back to original, distant and different sources, rather than taking short cuts by quoting and summarising other people's more recent books.

When researching the history of Maidenhead it is hard to resist the conclusion that the town has certainly missed out on some big opportunities in its time. There are four lost opportunities that immediately spring to mind, and they are as follows:

(1) How was it that Maidenhead once upon a time had a high-society racecourse that suddenly and mysteriously became an also ran, losing out to the nearby Royal Ascot racecourse that was opened by Queen Anne in 1711. It's not that the small village of Ascot was any more convenient for the royal family in residence at Windsor Castle, or that Maidenhead did not have a perfectly good racecourse of its own, which was, as we have seen, attended by George III and his family in the early 18th century. Yet little Ascot succeeded in putting Maidenhead's nose out of joint and there is no racecourse in Maidenhead today, as there might very well have been had things not gone wrong for Maidenhead. So what went wrong? Why Royal Ascot instead of Royal Maidenhead?

(2) The same question applies to the lost opportunity of a fashionable high-society regatta in Maidenhead, such as is held annually in Henley-upon-Thames. Why did Maidenhead not have a regatta of its own that might have held its own with nearby Henley? How come it fell behind here as well? There can be no doubt that Maidenhead had the same opportunities as Ascot and Henley-on-Thames, but it did not take them for some reason.

(3) At some point in the recording of its history, Maidenhead has neglected to record the names of its first and subsequent mayors. As we have seen, the town council did not know the name of the first Mayor of Maidenhead until the *Maidenhead Advertiser* and I paid attention to this, and

until the Windsor and Maidenhead librarian Chris Atkins got onto it. At some point there has been a lost opportunity here to record the details of the town's earliest mayors and to know more about them.

(4) And then there is the aforesaid lost opportunity of a history museum that never materialised in Maidenhead! Reading has a museum, but not Maidenhead. York has a Viking Museum, but there is no such museum in Maidenhead where there is a seriously interesting Viking history to tell. How come?

On the other hand, the history of Maidenhead is not just one of lost opportunities, as we have seen in these pages, and which town or city in the UK does not have a few missed opportunities of note? So never mind the missed opportunities, because much else has been gained that is entirely due to the enterprise and credit of Maidenhead, some of the key local developments of which, according to my thesis, have connected with and contributed to matters of national and occasionally international importance.

But how well does my thesis stand up?

It seems to me that it stands up as follows.

Maidenhead's most important national connections with and contributions to national history have been:

(1) Helping – along with the rest of Berkshire and Wessex – to defeat the Danish Vikings in England once and for all, and to restore the capital city of London to England, preventing it from becoming a Danish city and preventing England from becoming a Danish country.

(2) Helping London and the nation to connect with Bristol and Bath with the first all-important stepping stone in a Great Western Rail Network. Providing that network with the successful completion of the first railway station and the first railway bridge – the biggest of its kind in the country at that time – in a development that was of national importance, the success of which, in Maidenhead, was crucial to the provision of a launch pad into the west of England.

(3) Providing London with a similar launch pad in the days of horse-drawn coaches, when Maidenhead took the initiative and built a wooden bridge across the River Thames, which provided London and the nation

with a more direct route to Bristol and Bath than it would have had otherwise.

(4) Providing London with a 'gateway to the Thames' capable of trafficking 100 river boats per day at Boulter's Lock.

(5) Providing London and the nation with Britain's and the world's first successful flight of a vertical take-off aircraft (the Fairey Rotodyne) in 1957.

(6) Also in 1957, providing the nation with the first racing car to win a British Grand Prix since 1934 (the Vanwall, driven by Stirling Moss).

Here we have half a dozen examples of how Maidenhead's local history has connected with and contributed to national history, and this sheds a very different light on its local history. I was tempted to add the example of William Turner's famous painting of a train crossing Maidenhead Bridge – *Rain, Steam and Speed* – to this list because it is certainly an example of how Maidenhead has connected with the nation's art and culture and provided a suitable subject for it, not that this actually changed the progress of national history as the other events cited did, although it has given Maidenhead a place in the art history of the nation. To have inspired a national artist of international renown to come to the town and paint the biggest railway bridge in England is, of course, of national historical significance, and it does shed new light on the local history of Maidenhead, albeit without changing very much, like the half a dozen examples that I have singled out for consideration here.

Of course, these examples were driven by national policies, expertise and events – they were not locally driven – and they were also driven by inventions and a good deal of investment from elsewhere. They would have happened with or without the participation of Maidenhead – with the notable exception of the defeat of the Danish Vikings, which was a regional rather than a national event driven by Berkshire and Wessex as a whole – but the fact remains that Maidenhead was involved in the successful implementation of all these historical developments of national importance that would not have succeeded as well as they did had Maidenhead not played its part. I am not saying that these are the only examples of how Maidenhead has connected with or been touched by national history – as we have seen in this book there are other examples – but it seems to me that those detailed in this chapter are by far the most important. Kings and queens have been to Maidenhead for one reason or another, but that in itself has not seriously altered the course of history anywhere near as much as these other developments. These royal visits could just as easily have taken place elsewhere, and they didn't change or make much of a difference to anything, unlike the other life-changing events that have seriously affected the progress of British history because they were important milestones – defining moments. Of course, King William of Orange's soldiers came to Maidenhead to drive out Catholic Irish troops, and his new form of constitutional monarchy made a tremendous and very welcome difference to the progress of government, monarchy and democracy in Britain, but the king's men did not only come to Maidenhead, they went to many other places besides, and the king was well on his way to achieving his goal with or without any marginal assistance from Maidenhead. And although King Charles I was brought to Maidenhead as a prisoner of Oliver Cromwell to meet his children before he was beheaded, he was going to meet them somewhere with or without Maidenhead.

Half a dozen national connections of importance in the local history of a small country town may not sound very much compared with other bigger towns and cities, but when one considers the importance of these connections to the nation at large, and compares them with the connections and contributions of other small country towns, they are at least very startling, if not seriously impressive. Relatively speaking, Maidenhead has played quite an important part in national history thanks to its geographical location near to London and Windsor, and thanks to it having taken the initiative to place itself on a direct westerly route out of and into London (top marks to those Elentone and Pinkney's Green entrepreneurs who had the foresight and excellent sense of timing to build their wooden bridge where and when they did, to plant, as it were, their little acorn).

But what of Maidenhead's international connections?

They, too, are quite startling and show the local history of the town in an international as well as a local light. They have been as follows:

(1) Providing the outside world – and the US and Europe in particular – with an excellent example of how to build and operate an advanced

railway bridge, station and line, at a time when most of the outside world did not know how to do this. Providing this test-bed example to British India, likewise, at a time when the eyes of the Raj were on Britain and on Maidenhead to see how successful or otherwise these early railway developments were and whether they could be adopted in India, as they very soon were.

(2) Providing the outside world with a futuristic Flood Alleviation Scheme – the Jubilee River, the second biggest man-made river in Europe and the biggest in Britain – from which lessons can be learned in coping with the increasing incidence of devastating floods in the new millennium.

(3) Providing the outside world with the world's first vertical-aircraft flight, from which advances in aeronautical engineering have been made.

Here we have three impressive examples of how local history in Maidenhead has made international history – history of interest and importance to the world at large as well as to the nation, because the world at large can and indeed has learnt from events in Maidenhead once upon a time. Again, this sheds new light on the local history of Maidenhead and enables its townspeople to see themselves and their local history in a new light. But two of the above (with the exception of the Jubilee River) would have happened with or without the participation of Maidenhead – the investment and the expertise came from elsewhere – not that this alters the fact that it was with Maidenhead's participation that they did happen, and that the world has and can learn from this. And while the Jubilee River was a regional rather than a purely local development, it was a regional development in which Maidenhead played a crucial part. To connect with and contribute to world history in three important ways – in addition to connecting with and contributing to national history in half a dozen important ways – is not bad at all for a small country town, and it demonstrates the difference that local history can and does make to people's lives.

And there I rest my case.

I hope you have enjoyed reading this book as much as I have enjoyed writing it.

Bibliography

Adair, John *By the Sword Divided*, Book Club Associates, London, 1983.

Bayley, Harold *Archaic England*, Chapman & Hall, London, 1919.

Beckinsale, R.P. *Companion into Berkshire*, Methuen, London, 1951.

Belloc, Hilaire *The Historic Thames*, Webb & Bower (Michael Joseph), London, 1988.

Briggs, Asa *A Social History of England*, Book Club Associates, London, 1983.

Camden, William *Britannia*, John Stockdale, London, 1806.

Clunn, Harold *The Face of the Home Counties*, Simpkin Marshall, London, 1936.

Ditchfield, P.H. *Byways in Berkshire and The Cotswolds*, 1920.

Fraser, Antonia *The Weaker Vessel*, Methuen, London, 1984.

Hanks, Patrick *The Oxford Names Companion*, Oxford, 2002.

Hibbert, Christopher *The English: A Social History 1066–1945*. Book Club Associates, London, 1987

Law, Joy *The Hollow Crown*, History Book Club, London, 1971.

Muir, Richard *The Villages of England*, Thames & Hudson, London, 1992.

Savage, Anne *The Anglo-Saxon Chronicles*, Phillips/Heinemann, London, 1982.

Trevelyan, G.M. *English Social History*, Penguin Books, London, 1986.

Trevor-Roper, Hugh *Princes and Artists*, Thames and Hudson, 1991.

Wesley Walker, J. *A History of Maidenhead*, St Catherine Press, London, 1931.

Other Sources

Domesday Book, Complied by direction of King William I, Winchester, 1086.

The Anglo-Saxon Chronicles, Volumes One and Two, London, Longman, 1861.

The Chilterns & The Thames Valley, Bell & Sons, 1932.

The National Dictionary of Biography, Oxford University Press, Oxford, 2006.

Royal Windsor & Maidenhead Library and Education Department, Windsor, 2006.

Maidenhead Advertiser, Maidenhead, special editions January & February 1890.

Maidenhead Heritage Centre, Maidenhead, 2006.